Preston North End

The Sixties

Edward Skingsley

DEDICATION

This book is dedicated to my daughters, Catherine and Elizabeth, who have never really understood my enthusiasm for our hometown club. Opting to spend their formative years with 'Beanie Babies' or even raising a cyber pet on a 'Tamagotchi' pendant rather than suffer alongside me at Deepdale was, on reflection, a sound decision to make for children of such tender years. That shrewdness has blossomed further over the years; their accomplishments so far have been many and leave me with more than a touch of pride.

CONTENTS

Continued...

Continued...

Continued...

ACKNOWLEDGMENTS

Preston North End Football Club with thanks to Ben Rhodes
Lancashire Evening Post with thanks to Mike Hill
Hammers Ex Magazine with thanks to Tony McDonald
Kevin Williamson with special thanks
John Steinson with special thanks
Bob Bond
Kenneth Berry
Yorkshire Post Newspapers
Express Newspapers
Mirror Newspapers

I THE SIXTIES

At the very end of the Sixties, Deepdale probably - using the parlance of the time - wasn't really the 'cool' place to 'hang out' even for any self respecting North End fan. In fact, it was probably as bleak an option as it was at the very start of the decade when North End were promptly relegated in the season following Tom Finney's retirement. Many of the faithful fan base 'retired' with Finney, and the grim reality was that those *'power in the land'* heydays were finally over.

After walking the Division Two plank in 1969/70, the last thing that sprang to mind back then were the stout deeds achieved by the many players that had represented the club in those ten years of massive social change. It's only as time marches on that one appreciates that North End actually succeeded in achieving some great results with some thrilling displays.

The bulk of these outstanding performances occurred as 'runs' in the FA Cup that were studded in clusters across the whole decade, peaking of course with a memorable appearance in the 1964 Final. That season also represented North End's best attempt to escape from Division Two finishing a very creditable third, behind Leeds United and Sunderland.

The season ended in disappointment though when reality finally dawned on the North End fans that despite being FA Cup runners-up and Division Two 'bridesmaids,' a season of high excitement and anticipation had resulted in nothing more than going back to 'square one.'

During the Sixties many players of great talent played in North End's colours. The North End youth policy delivered names such as Peter Thompson, George Ross, Howard Kendall, Alan Spavin, Tony Singleton and Dave Wilson for free. To that add other notable imports such as Alan Kelly, Alex Dawson, Nobby Lawton, Alec Ashworth, Brian Godfrey, Ernie Hannigan, George Lyall, Derek Temple, Jim McNab, Ken Knighton, Graham Hawkins, Willie Irvine and Archie Gemmill, and you have a talent pool that should have gained so much more success whilst they were at Deepdale, rather than just pass through its corridors.

1960/61
Division One: Finished 22nd – Relegated along with Newcastle United
FA Cup: 4th Round – Defeated by Swansea Town 2-1 (a)
League Cup: 3rd Round – Defeated by Aston Villa 3-1 after replay (a)

1961/62
Division Two: Finished 10th.
FA Cup: Quarter Final – Defeated by Manchester Utd 2-1 after replay (a)
League Cup: 3rd Round – Defeated by Rotherham Utd 3-0 after replay (a)

1962/63
Division Two: Finished 16th
FA Cup: 3rd Round – Defeated by Sunderland 1-4 (h)
League Cup: 4th Round – Defeated 6-2 by Aston Villa (a)

1963/64
Division Two: Finished 3rd behind Leeds Utd and Sunderland
FA Cup: Final – Defeated by West Ham Utd 3-2
League Cup: 2nd Round – Defeated by Newcastle Utd 3-0 (a)

1964/65
Division Two: Finished 12th
FA Cup: 4th Round – Defeated by Bolton Wanderers 1-2 (h)
League Cup: 2nd Round – Defeated by Doncaster Rovers 1-0 (a)

1965/66
Division Two: Finished 17th
FA Cup: Quarter Final – Defeated by Manchester Utd 3-1 after replay (a)
League Cup: 4th Round – Defeated by Grimsby Town 4-0 (a)

1966/67
Division Two: Finished 13th
FA Cup: 3rd Round – Defeated by Aston Villa 0-1 (h)
League Cup: 3rd Round – Defeated by Leeds Utd 3-0 after replay (a)

1967/68
Division Two: Finished 20th
FA Cup: 4th Round – Defeated by Tottenham Hotspur 3-1 (a)
League Cup: 2nd Round – Defeated by Oxford Utd 2-1 (a)

1968/69
Division Two: Finished 14th
FA Cup: 4th Round – Defeated by Chelsea after replay 2-1 (a)
League Cup: 2nd Round – Defeated by Crystal Palace 3-1 (a)

1969/70
Division Two: Finished 22nd relegated along with Aston Villa
FA Cup: 3rd Round – Defeated by Derby County after replay 4-1 (a)
League Cup: 1st Round – Defeated by Bury 0-1 (h)

There were some appalling defeats along the ten year journey, but there were also some sensational victories, and some of those very much against the odds.

Jimmy Milne, from Dundee and a North End player in the 'glory days,' was the man at the managerial helm for the bulk of the sixties. He had taken over from Cliff Britton in 1961 and remained in charge until 'moving upstairs' to accommodate Bobby Seith becoming first team coach in 1968.

Seith, appreciated and well respected by all the players, soldiered on until April 1970 when he was sacked after a disastrous season. He was unfortunate that his time at the helm was hampered by a board that was beholden to the bank.

I get the impression after speaking to older fans that even without Finney, everyone thought that it would just be a matter of time before Proud Preston were back amongst the elite. It's now 55 years and counting...

2 FAREWELL, SPECIAL ONE

PRESTON NORTH END 2 LUTON TOWN 0
DIVISION ONE 30/4/1960

It's only fitting that we begin North End's journey through the sixties by paying homage to their most famous son – Sir Tom Finney.

Sir Tom retired just as the sixties began, after a brilliant career for both club and country. Despite having a reasonably talented team around him, he was the real reason North End were one of the nation's foremost teams in the late forties and into the fifties.

Sir Tom's last competitive game for North End took place on the final day of the 1959/60 season at Deepdale, against Luton Town. It was a lovely spring day weather wise, and everything to make it memorable happened, except for that elusive goal for the man of the moment which would have made it the *perfect day*.

The chance to say goodbye to North End's finest swelled the crowd to 29,781 - and what a great send off he got.

Both the North End and Luton Town teams lined up in a guard of honour formation as Tom took to the field of play, before linking arms and singing along with the crowd 'Auld Lang Syne' and 'For He's a Jolly Good Fellow!'

An emotionally choked Finney was wearing his famous No.7 shirt again too, giving the faithful one last glimpse of their hero on the right wing. Although not a single spectator left Deepdale before the final whistle, the match itself wasn't vintage. Being there and celebrating this most poignant of occasions was what made this day memorable.

The North End team was:-

Else, Wilson, Walton, Fullham, Dunn, Smith, Finney, Milne, Alston, Sneddon and Taylor.

The pitch was dry, firm and ultimately hard to conquer that day. Finney was less than 100% fit too, but eventually gave the crowd something to remember him by.

North End went 1-0 ahead in the 35th minute thanks to Alec Alston, and that's how it remained until half time. Finney seemed within himself, and later admitted the emotion of the occasion had got to him.

It didn't stop him laying on the second North End goal just after the interval though, Finney putting Jim Smith through to score.

As the match went into its last quarter, Finney seemed to give it everything he had, and gave the crowd more than a glimpse of the old magic culminating in a missed chance after leaving two defenders chasing his shadow.

The Greatest

Too soon it was all over and a podium was hurriedly brought on for Finney to mount and speak to the North End crowd who had idolised him, week in and week out for 14 years. With voice trembling he said,

"I hardly know what to say, it's such a sad, sad day for me. I would like to thank you all for the wonderful support I have enjoyed during my time here, and also for the many tributes paid to me in letters from all over England. I would like to thank the North End directors and my colleagues for making it such a wonderful time while I have been at Deepdale. It is sad, but today is a day I will remember forever and thank you all for making it so grand."

Sir Tom's niece, Michelle Peacock, remembers him as, *"Just a really nice uncomplicated man, nothing was ever too much trouble for him. If someone wanted to say a few words to him or wanted his autograph they were never turned away wherever it was."*

It's fantastic that Preston North End can boast that this gentleman and giant of the game was theirs. He meant so much to so many. We will never see his like again.

From the archives: The goalkeeper is left helpless as Finney powers home a flying header

3   THE FIRST FLUSH OF YOUTH

PRESTON NORTH END 1 CHELSEA 4 (SECOND LEG) 3/5/1960
FA YOUTH TROPHY FINAL

Within a few days of losing the legendary Tom Finney to retirement, the North End fans had the chance to glimpse into the future and see how the very promising youth team would perform in the second leg of the 1959/60 FA Youth Trophy Final.

They had done extremely well to date, vanquishing Wigan, Huddersfield, Liverpool, Durham County, Birmingham, Swansea and Manchester United in an epic semi final. United had been winners of the competition in five of the previous seven years.

The first leg of the final was held at Stamford Bridge. The Chelsea team, bristling with future internationals, were expected to see off the outsiders from Deepdale. However, despite having most of the game, they could only force a draw after North End took a shock lead in the 85th minute.

David Wilson started the move and fed the ball to Peter Thompson. Progressing towards goal while easing past a couple of defenders, his run was inadvertently interrupted by teammate Ian Matthews. Thompson unselfishly let Matthews carry on, and within a matter of seconds the ball was being fished out of the back of the Chelsea net.

Back slapping all round was instantly followed by a lapse in youthful concentration as the Chelsea surge forward immediately bore long overdue fruit. John Hart, in the middle of the North End defence, failed to clear the ball cleanly and it glanced to the ever dangerous Bert Murray. Brushing aside Rodney Webb's challenge, Murray took his chance superbly by ramming the ball home past John Barton in the North End goal.

North End just about hung on until the end of this first leg, but it's interesting to note the general press view that night on some of the North End 'lads,' who along with goalkeeper Barton would go on to rack up well over 1,200 North End first team appearances between them...

Alan Spavin – *"...was Preston's outstanding player"*

Peter Thompson – *"...has pace and strength"*

David Wilson – *"...covered two positions very effectively"*

George Ross – *"...like a rock in defence, inspiring performance"*

After the echoing sound of the small 9,037 crowd in the massive Stamford Bridge arena, the football public of Preston paid a much more appreciative tribute to their young, enthusiastic team with 27,744 turning up to watch the second leg at Deepdale.

The teams were :-

North End
Barton, Ross, Webb, Baldwin, Will, Hart, Smith, Wilson, Thompson, Spavin and Matthews.
Chelsea
Bonetti, Butler, Harris, Venables, More, Carney, Murray, Shaw, Bolland, Tambling and Robinson.

Alas, it wasn't to be a wonderful evening. Chelsea chose this night to demonstrate their obvious class and power. Coached by the renowned Ted Drake, the trio of Terry Venables, Peter Bonetti and Bobby Tambling - all with first team experience - saw to it that the contest wasn't even close.

Venables owned the midfield. His passing and foresight were a joy to watch and caused the hosts much anxiety; in contrast North End tended to dither and get caught in possession, severely limiting their forward progress.

Dominating from the start with the obvious aim of taking an early lead, Chelsea set to work.

After the visitors won a corner on the left on 11 minutes, Venables took control and flicked the ball sideways to Tambling directly from the quadrant. The inside forwards' full blooded rising drive could only be touched by Barton as it flew into the top corner of the net.

The pattern had been set. Four minutes later, Chelsea won a free kick just outside the North End box and again Venables appeared on the scene, pointing hither and thither to add extra confusion to the already overrun North End defence. He then sidestepped the free kick, allowing the ball through to Tambling once again, who buried the ball into the North End net past the unsighted Barton.

North End were clearly rattled, kicking the ball anywhere to get it away from their penalty area. Thompson was the only saving grace for North End at this point, holding the ball up and looking for work.

He played a big part in helping transform the game somewhat after Chelsea's second, developing a move well with Spavin, whose chip to Matthews saw the youngster thump home a great goal past the leaping Bonetti.

With the crowd now behind them, North End drove forward as never before and shots from Thompson and Michael Smith went just wide. The speed of Chelsea's breaks when regaining the ball were difficult for North End to repel and the visitors, without too many further dramas, got back on top.

Half time arrived with no further addition to the scoreline however, and the North End followers still had hope. It was false hope. Chelsea, as champions do, never slackened their grip for the remainder of the match.

On the hour, Colin Shaw tested Barton with a snap shot then David Will made a defensive slip, which brought another Chelsea forward, Gordon Bolland, into play. Racing in to gain full control, he drew Barton before lashing home a powerful shot.

Chelsea were now burning bright, and just ten minutes later added another superb goal. Tambling, as alert as ever, turned a defender's indecision into a splendidly taken fourth goal.

The final whistle sounded to prolonged appreciative applause from the Preston public, not only for their own team who had played so well throughout the tournament, but also to Chelsea who demonstrated a high level of football skill to deservedly lift the trophy.

The Preston North End 1960 FA Youth Trophy Final squad

Back Row: Ross, Webb, Baldwin, Barton, Will, Laing, Hart.
Front Row: Smith, Wilson, Thompson, Spavin, Humes, Matthews.

4   INTO THE CAULDRON

LIVERPOOL 0 PRESTON NORTH END 0
FA CUP 5TH ROUND 17/2/1962

"Liverpool... will play Preston North End," said the resolute voice in the background of the FA headquarters in Lancaster Gate, London. The third and fourth balls drawn had produced an all Division Two clash in the fifth round of the FA Cup in 1962.

Liverpool were the immediate and obvious favourites to go through as they were enjoying a tremendous promotion drive and leading the table under new manager Bill Shankly's guidance. The bookies registered North End as 100/1 outsiders to win the cup, while Liverpool were offered at 10/1. Bookies aren't often wrong are they.......?

North End had begun their FA Cup campaign with a 3-2 third round victory at home to Watford, notable in the main for the last-kick-of-the-match penalty save by Alan Kelly that ended 'The Hornets' interest for another year.

It was a heart stopping moment for fans of both teams. With the chance of a replay riding on the free shot, Tony Gregory strode up and placed the ball on the penalty spot.

Alan Kelly himself explained best what happened next. *"Gregory tried to place his shot. I went down to my left. The ball hit me but then span upwards. I completely lost sight of the ball for a second or two but turned round on the floor and caught the ball on the line."* The final whistle was then blown. What a contrast in fortunes between Kelly and

Gregory. Kelly, mobbed by his teammates and Gregory, walking slowly from the pitch head bowed.

The reward for the win was another home tie - this time against Southern League Weymouth.

The 'Terras' player manager would need no introduction to the North End faithful - he was none other than Frank O'Farrell, who had only left Deepdale in the previous close season to sample his first taste of football management in sleepy Dorset.

The first attempt to settle this tie on January 27th lasted just 14 minutes. That was when referee, Mr Langdale from Darlington, signaled he had 'seen enough' - well, paradoxically speaking anyway. The blanket of mist that was present at the kick off had transformed into a 'pea souper' and was getting worse. This was a massive blow to Weymouth's 1,300 supporters who had journeyed up all the way up from the south coast. It was back to Preston Station for them, while Weymouth FC tagged a couple of extra days onto their Blackpool hotel tab.

The game started again on Monday evening, and resulted in a 2-0 win for the Lilywhites. In front a crowd of just over 26,000, North End dominated the game; the visitors best spell coming in the early exchanges.

Weymouth's keeper, Billy Bly, was the character of the team and at 41 years of age had returned from retirement (after 23 years of protecting the Hull City net) by answering an emergency 'Goalkeeper Needed' appeal by Frank O'Farrell earlier that year. Prepared to make the 500 mile round trip for every home game, Bly was certainly determined to enjoy himself at Deepdale.

He did well, as his frantic string of last ditch saves were directly proportionate to North End's dominance. The breakthrough finally came just before half time, after a catalogue of errors in the visitor's penalty area.

Alfie Briggs lobbed the ball forward into the Weymouth box and Bly mis-punched the ball. Centre half Tony Hobson attempting to clear on the line sliced the ball back high into the air and Alex Dawson dispatched a header back towards the unmanned goal. Agonisingly for Bly, his flailing fingertips couldn't stop the ball rolling into the net.

Bly was both blameless and powerless to stop the second, tie clinching goal, however. Peter Thompson bore down on full back John Shepherd, beating him with ease. Cutting infield, he released an explosive right foot shot that Bly could only watch sail past him and into the net.

Any possibility of a Weymouth rally was nipped in the bud by the North End defence, led well by Tony Singleton, with full backs Willie Cunningham and George Ross particularly strong.

The first match up in the epic trilogy of the North End v Liverpool games took place at Anfield on February 17th 1962. Although this tie was contested between two Second Division teams, the interest in both the town and city involved in the preceding days was enormous.

Liverpool, sitting proudly at the top of the division, had amassed 42 points from their 28 games to date, having rattled in 67 goals in the process. North End were tenth, with 30 goals less to their credit. How would North End live with the international Liverpool forward line of Roger Hunt, Alan A'Court, Ian St John and Ian Callaghan? The form book pointed the inquisitive fan firmly towards the red corner.....

Anfield was absolutely bulging - and deafening - as the two teams made their way onto the pitch. North End took the field with :-

Kelly, Cunningham, Ross, Wylie, Singleton, Smith, Wilson, Biggs, Dawson, Spavin and Thompson

It was certainly a relief to see Dawson and Singleton run down the tunnel, as their fitness had been in doubt all week.

With the crowd officially registered at 54,967, Liverpool won the toss and defended the Kop end, as was their choice in those days. They saw driving forward towards a packed and swaying Kop in the second half a distinct advantage over the cowering opposition - and who could argue?

By the end of the 61/62 season they would score 68 league goals at Anfield alone.

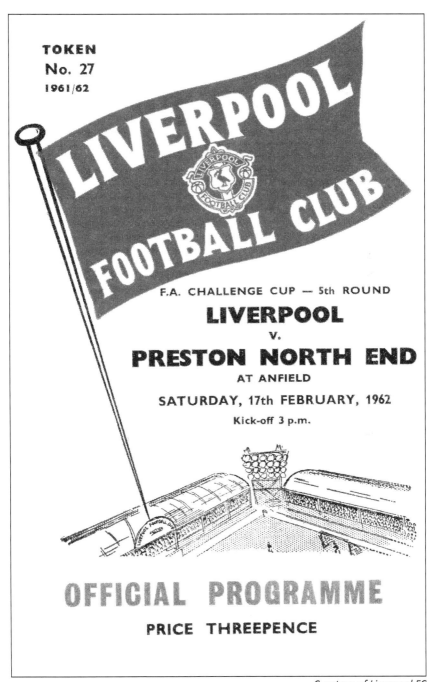

TOKEN
No. 27
1961/62

LIVERPOOL
FOOTBALL CLUB

F.A. CHALLENGE CUP — 5th ROUND

LIVERPOOL
V.
PRESTON NORTH END

AT ANFIELD

SATURDAY, 17th FEBRUARY, 1962

Kick-off 3 p.m.

OFFICIAL PROGRAMME

PRICE THREEPENCE

Courtesy of Liverpool FC

Back Row: Dawson, Ross, Singleton, Kelly, Smith, Alston, Wylie.   Front Row: Wilson, Biggs, Cunningham, Spavin, Thompson.

The committed and resolute North End squad who took Liverpool the distance over three epic FA Cup ties in 1962

The two managers involved, Shankly and Milne, went back a long way. Both Scots, they were the North End half backs for quite some time in the same team, but now all that friendship was set aside - just for the length of the game, of course!

In the early exchanges it was surprisingly North End who were keeping the Kop quiet and a little anxious with the speed of their raids down the flanks. Tom Leishman, the Liverpool half back, also felt nervous enough to intercept an Alex Dawson cross that Bert Slater was about to catch and head out for a corner. Dawson took his position in the middle of the box, but the ball was cleared by Ron Yeats, by now apparently glued at the hip to the big centre forward.

Patient play from Preston eventually saw a couple more headers from Jim Smith and Alfie Biggs safely collected by Slater. It had been a very bright few minutes from Preston, but now play swung at a frantic pace to the other end.

Accompanied by an elevated roar from the Liverpool faithful, the home side put a few moves of their own together. Two crosses were pumped in from wide, but Tony Singleton towered above the target, Ian St John, with some ease and cleared them away. Roger Hunt then got involved in a passing interchange with Liverpool winger, Alan A'Court, putting him in the clear down the middle, but his shot ballooned wide as he lost his footing.

It was all very fast and furious now, North End responding through Biggs who embarked on a barnstorming run at goal, eventually meeting the brick wall, otherwise known as Yeats. The play swung back; Gordon Milne's low drive at goal was charged down by Smith and only partially cleared, then Willie Cunningham blocked a goal bound shot only for the clearance to land at the feet of Hunt. Fortunately for North End, Hunt couldn't control the ball and it went out for a goal kick.

The gathering excitement continued. On 11 minutes, North End shook Liverpool and the Kop, when Dawson put the ball into the net via the post following a rapid breakaway instigated by David Wilson. Progressing at pace, he passed inside to Biggs who in turn fed Dawson. However, the goal was contentiously disallowed for offside - the flag only being raised when the ball entered the net. In fact, Dawson had actually paused upon collecting the pass from Biggs and seeing no flag raised, had continued his run.

North End had definitely seen the better of the first 15 minutes, and continued to worry Liverpool whenever they moved forward. Slater was tested to the full again by Dawson after his 20 yard drive seemed to gather pace as it homed in on goal.

Liverpool attacked again, the ball eventually landing perfectly in the 'D' for Roger Hunt to execute a great shot on target, but Alan Kelly was aware and correctly positioned to deal with it.

Biggs was racing forward at every opportunity and a superb centre on the run saw Dawson out jump Yeats, the header just dropping over the bar.

For all their bright play, North End almost went one down on 20 minutes. Leishman intercepted a loose defensive pass by Wilson and careered forward towards the North End goal quite impressively, but his final shot lacked power and was food and drink for the advancing Kelly.

Wilson made amends immediately. Flying down the right and cutting in, he was 'stopped' in no uncertain terms by the embarrassed Ronnie Moran, who simply couldn't keep up with him. The winger immediately took the free kick and drove it hard, low and dangerously across the face of the Liverpool goal, but there wasn't a North Ender far enough forward to apply the finishing touch.

North End were certainly battering the Liverpool door, but it was standing firm. A true battle of cut and thrust, incident and mobility was being served up for an appreciative crowd.

A Liverpool free kick 30 yards out almost took North End by surprise. It was teed up for Yeats whose thunderbolt shot with all the weight of his frame behind it, whistled past the left post, with Kelly motionless.

Moran was tormented again by Wilson, whose pass inside allowed Biggs to launch a terrific shot that just curled over the Liverpool bar. A few minutes later, a corner taken by Wilson was perfectly dispatched to meet the onrushing John Wylie's head - the ball cannoning off a stationary and bemused Moran for another corner.

At the other end, the crowd noise elevated as Singleton had to be spoken to by the referee for his overzealous attempts to prise the ball away from St John, who lay prostrate on the floor.

Despite the attentions of the quick moving Liverpool forward line, Preston had stood firm and were not bending. As the whistle blew, nobody could really argue that the first half clearly belonged to North End.

The Kop's presence was soon felt after the restart. Every time the home team moved forward towards the assembled throng, a deafening roar of anticipation helped them along their way.

However, as in the first half, it was North End who threatened first, but Wilson's cross to Spavin was slightly over hit and the young midfielder was always struggling to reach the ball - his off balance header failing to trouble Slater.

North End then followed this up with a slick move that almost brought them the lead. Spavin played the ball quickly wide to the productive Wilson. The wingers' pass inside was quickly made to the on running Biggs, whose shot 'on the fly' was executed to perfection. With Slater helpless, the ball flashed just inches over the bar.

North End were more than holding their own in this cauldron of noise and Dawson suffered the frustration of having a second goal disallowed in the 52nd minute.

Spavin broke forward and headed directly down the middle towards the Liverpool box catching Yeats - Dawson's chaperone for the day - in a state of complete indecision. All alone, the giant defender wanted to challenge Spavin but didn't want to unshackle himself from Dawson. In the end as he moved forwards, Spavin threaded the ball through to Dawson who unceremoniously drove the ball into the net.

There was much dismay all round for the visiting team and fans, as the bright yellow linesman's flag was then spotted raised high in front of gleeful Liverpool fans.

Peter Thompson, who had been well patrolled by his allotted marker Gerry Byrne, was stopped by Milne who passed the ball quickly through the North End midfield to set up a breakaway down the right wing.

With the Kop loud, animated and swaying to and fro, A'Court raced forward with the ball finding Callaghan with a neat pass. His fierce low drive was saved by Kelly at the foot of the post, to the relief of the North End fans all with their hearts in their mouths. It was easy to see now how teams defending the Kop end were intimidated into making mistakes...

Panic set in yet again in the North End penalty box when a hurried clearance rebounded to Hunt off Singleton, around ten yards out. Hunt controlled the ball and his lobbed shot beat Kelly's flailing dive, only to gently hit the bar and rebound into play. There then followed an almighty scramble for possession with captain Cunningham fearlessly getting involved and taking a heavy blow - the resulting foul relieving the pressure.

In fact, the veteran Cunningham was the epitome of calmness and control, breaking up many developing Liverpool moves. He was certainly unshakeable, with his attitude of 'been there, done that' a real plus point for North End.

The game continued at breakneck speed.

Yeats was in the thick of the action at both ends. As time was running out, he appeared more and more in the North End box hoping to finally convert a winner for his team. On one such occasion, he powerfully met an A'Court corner only to see it whizz inches over the bar with Kelly rooted. The Kop thought that was the moment; rivers of fans moved forward down the packed terracing before returning to whence they came.

The big defender was then required in his own box, struggling manfully to shepherd Dawson away from a lightly hit back pass to Slater.

North End had time for one more tilt at Liverpool. Biggs made yet another forward burst and teed up Dawson. The resulting pile driver was deflected - and desperately so - wide of the post...by that man

Yeats.

The referee finally brought this epic contest to a close, North End being by far the happier team.

It was all still to play for in the replay at Deepdale the following Tuesday evening, as the North End faithful filed out of Anfield.

Returning home to the old bus station on Tithebarn Street via a veritable fleet of those double decker *'Ribble', 'Scout'* and *'Standerwick'* buses, many had smiles on their faces.

5 THRILLER

PRESTON NORTH END 0 LIVERPOOL 0
FA CUP 5TH ROUND REPLAY 20/2/1962

On Monday lunchtime, it was time for the FA Cup quarter final draw. North End were seventh out of the velvet bag. North End or Liverpool would have to play Manchester United or Sheffield Wednesday.

This was a great spur for North End. Somehow dispose of Liverpool and it could be Matt Busby's Manchester United at Deepdale!

North End were expecting a 35,000 crowd for the Liverpool replay the following evening. Long queues were snaking around Deepdale for tickets well before 7am on Monday morning, and never diminished in size all day.

A little bit of 'needle' between the two clubs had been thrown into the mix since the final whistle at Anfield. An obviously frustrated Liverpool manager, Bill Shankly, had accused North End of 'stifling and spoiling' the game and *only wanting a draw* when asked by the press for his post match opinion.

It was hard to see where he was coming from with such an outburst. Surely, he didn't expect a self respecting North End to turn up at Anfield and happily go the way of so many before them in what had become a graveyard for visiting teams?

 The national press had all seemed impressed with North End's resilient performance, indeed North End felt moved to maintain that their play in the first encounter didn't warrant such criticism in what was a typical cup tie.

Preston was in a traffic meltdown situation a couple of hours before the replay was due to kick off. Heavy traffic from all directions saw to it that many thousands didn't even make it to the ground, never mind spend over two hours trying to make their way home after it had finished. It is recorded that the Liverpool team coach arrived at 7:32 pm, escorted by two police cars and two motor cycle patrolmen. The referee gave the visitors a further 20 minutes to get themselves together and ready to play.

In fact, Mr Kevin Howley, the match referee, was getting rather anxious himself. His linesmen only managed to arrive at 7:15 pm, by which time he had already started to coach a couple of deputies!

I have seen the crowd logged as both 37,825 and 37,831. Either way, they are wildly inaccurate - as anyone there that night will tell you. Gates lifted off their hinges, turnstiles leapfrogged, walls scaled - you name it - desperate fans were getting into Deepdale from all directions.

Climbing onto the floodlight pylons, hanging from stanchions, clinging to anything they could - *this* was the occasion when Preston North End's home crowd record was set! Both teams remained unchanged following the Anfield epic.

As early as the first minute, North End could have gone ahead. Biggs, picking up from where he had left off at Anfield, ran down the left and crossed for Wilson in the clear. Unfortunately, the winger hurried his header and the ball landed on top of the net rather than in it.

Dawson then missed a great opportunity in the 23rd minute to put North End in front when he completely mistimed a shot from around the penalty spot. Energised by this, North End hit a mini purple patch, five minutes of lovely football culminating in Biggs arrowing a shot just over the bar.

However, North End got lucky in the 35th minute. A Hunt shot had beaten Kelly and it was Cunningham who heroically hoofed the ball off the line to save the day.

As the half progressed, Hunt was looking the most potent of the Liverpool forwards. Twice in quick succession he shot narrowly wide and then ballooned another attempt high into the crowd.

Singleton firmly had St John in his pocket...again. The big North End centre half towered over the striker should Liverpool cross in the air, and to get a hefty boot in first if passed to feet.

Thompson was having an active game this time around. Somehow, Liverpool couldn't shackle him and he was creating opening after opening; alas none producing the vital goal.

North End had a little more of the play in the second half than their visitors, but were still fluffing their chances. Thompson put Dawson through after a wonderful run and pass, but with the goal at his mercy the big centre forward shot high and wide, much to the home fans disappointment.

Slater was busy. He stopped with great efficiency shots from Wilson and Dawson and another fierce drive from Cunnigham, the North End skipper.

Cunningham was having a fine game. He had taken part in these type of games many times and was delivering a master class in sure footed, controlled defending.

With the energy sapping prospect of extra time looming, Slater kept the Liverpool sheet clean with smart saves from Biggs and Dawson.

This contest had developed into a war of nerves, a mighty conflict between two teams not prepared to yield. With extra time about to start, overcoming tiredness, both mental and physical, were now thrown into the Deepdale melting pot.

It was Liverpool who dominated the first half of extra time. North End's younger players were feeling the strain but rejuvenated Liverpool could not beat Kelly. Singleton and Wylie came to the rescue with last gasp interventions. Callaghan had two attempts brilliantly saved by Kelly and it was the redoubtable Cunningham who stopped a dangerous raid singlehandedly, coming away with the ball to a round of loud applause.

The second half of extra time saw North End on the front foot again. Thompson weaved his way through the Liverpool defence only to slice his shot off target.

However, it was North End wing half Wylie, who had the home fans gasping for air as he felled Liverpool midfielder Jimmy Melia in what could only have been inches from the North End penalty area. Fortuitously, the free kick came to nothing and the exciting climax to this contest switched to the other end.

Jim Smith, North End's left half, hit a loose ball unexpectedly but with some venom at the Liverpool goal. The shot picked up a deflection on the way, and Slater hurriedly changing direction, just managed to parry the ball away for a corner while crashing into the foot of the post.

With a deafening noise behind them, North End launched a second all-out offensive to settle the issue.

The ball found Dawson not far out and he launched a hard accurate shot that went past the badly placed Slater and was heading for the unattended net, to the point where his fellow forwards had their arms raised in celebration. The Manchester United players, brought along by Matt Busby to watch their potential opponents from the stands, were all on their feet too, convinced their old friend had settled the issue.

With the ball about to cross the line, the covering full back Moran, unceremoniously pulled the jubilation rug from under the feet of the North End team and fans by sticking out a rock steady foot to deflect the ball to safety.

The Liverpool throng behind that Town End goal audibly gasped with relief, and so ended the second act, in what was now to become a trilogy.

Two hundred and ten minutes of thrills, spills, excitement, fear, but not a single goal, would now see the contestants play out another battle in six days time on a neutral ground – Old Trafford, Manchester.

As mentioned earlier, making the way home after the match proved more than difficult for many. It just added to the misery for some that thousands of away fans needed to cut across town to pick up the A59 towards Liverpool.

POST, WEDNESDAY, FEBRUARY 21, 1962.

North End battle through another thriller

By WALTER PILKINGTON

NORTH END are still in the Cup; in fact, but for a matter of inches near the end of last night's thrill-packed marathon fifth round replay with Liverpool at Deepdale, Preston would have earned the distinction of reaching the quarter finals. In quick succession Liverpool's goal had two dramatic escapes through which a sporting, cleanly fought contest retained a peal of nerve-racking tension.

As things developed, honours were even, and everyone was satisfied. Neither side really deserved to lose.

In the first of these late incidents suddenly a keenly headed...... by Liverpool had originally......

A FINE area at the foot of this......

One frustrated soul on that route felt moved to write an anguished letter to the *Lancashire Evening Post* about the whole sorry experience a couple of days later.

Describing the difficulty in getting back home to Hutton - *"usually a hop, skip and a jump away from Deepdale"* - as :-

"...trying to get out of a car park with no beginning or end, full of discourteous arm waving drivers," to then be, *"cross examined by a 'curler adorned' wife waiting in the darkness of the living room,"* wasn't what Mr D had bargained for...

"She didn't want to know about the late kick off, or the traffic chaos and least of all how we had played. I saved my breath and took a brew with me up to the spare bedroom after she dismissed my pleas, forcefully suggesting in a shrill voice that perhaps I should contact Yuri Gagarin for a lift home next time..."

Oh dear, oh dear, oh dear...

6   DELIVERANCE

LIVERPOOL 0 PRESTON NORTH END 1
FA CUP 5TH ROUND 2ND REPLAY 26/2/1962

Between the first and second replays against Liverpool, North End had to travel down to Eastville to play Bristol Rovers in a league encounter.

The match was lost 2-1, and for any fans hoping that North End's superb displays in the their two previous outings against Liverpool would kick start a league revival, a reality check was due.

With wing halves Smith and Wylie rested, very little enthusiasm was evident and it was no surprise when Rovers took the lead in the 21st minute. Although Biggs equalised with a great shot soon after, North End had hardly time to rearrange the elastic at the top of their shorts at the restart before they were picking the ball out of their net.

Despite Wilson's best efforts - he hit the post with a great shot – North End showed no sign of being finely tuned for their third meeting with Liverpool, due to kick off in around 48 hours time.

The last Monday of February, 1962 was in weather terms, dreadful. Snow had been falling on and off for a day but was now accompanied with a stiff freezing cold wind. Not the ideal weather to play out a massive and significant FA Cup tie in.

Peter Thompson had been due to make his England U23 debut against Scotland on this very day, but had asked for a release and expressed hope that this wouldn't harm his future England prospects.

**MANCHESTER
UNITED
FOOTBALL CLUB**

UNITED REVIEW

F.A. Cup – 5th Round
(2nd Replay)

**LIVERPOOL
v.
PRESTON**

Kick-off 7-30 pm

MONDAY
26th FEBRUARY

2d.

NUMBER 23
SPECIAL ISSUE

OFFICIAL SEASON 1961-62 **PROGRAMME**

WELCOME TO LIVERPOOL AND PRESTON

On behalf of the directors and staff of Manchester United Football Club, I offer a very hearty welcome to two of Lancashire's best-known and respected clubs – Liverpool and Preston. After 210 minutes in which neither side has scored a goal our friends tonight will make a third bid to reach the quarter-finals of this season's F.A. Cup Competition.

Everyone here tonight has a great interest in the result for obvious reasons and the followers of the fortunes of Manchester United particularly so.

It is always a pleasure to witness such a match between all-Lancashire rivals, especially when the outcome is of such great importance, and a second replay of a Fifth Round tie is certainly all of that.

The match brings Alex Dawson back to familiar territory once again . . . and these teams contain many familiar – and famous – names to football fans all over the country.

But two names missing from tonight's programme are those of Tom Finney (Preston) and Billy Liddell (Liverpool). These famous forwards have long and illustrious associations with the only clubs they served in professional football.

Both these great players have only recently retired from the "active list"; both were a credit to our National game and models of sportsmanship. Each won international honours, but it is for faithful service to their clubs that they will always be remembered in British football.

Tonight, I feel sure, we can look forward to a top-class match. If those on duty tonight can aspire to the heights of the two men I've mentioned and the many others who have worn the colours of their clubs in the past we will not be disappointed this evening in looking forward to an entertaining, well-contested match.

MATT BUSBY,
Manager M.U.F.C.

Courtesy of United Review

28

Reassured by England coach Walter Winterbottom that he had nothing to worry about in that respect, the 19 year old took his place on the North End team bus.

Just as physically arriving at Deepdale had been a problem for Liverpool last time out, now it was North End's turn.

The bus bravely set off from Deepdale – destination Old Trafford – well in time considering snow storms that were plaguing the locality. By the time it had reached Chorley, it had broken down and the driver was calling base from a telephone box asking for a replacement...and quick!

Players and officials duly transferred, the replacement bus set off but also ran into difficulty; the windscreen wiper mechanism freezing up in the bitter conditions. Eventually a flashing light police escort saw to it that the Lilywhites would be there in time for the kick off.

In spite of the bitterly cold conditions, a crowd of 43,944 clicked through the turnstiles. The pitch had a thin carpet of snow, hardening in the freezing wind. The teams were once again unchanged.

Despite his enthusiasm, Thompson was carrying a thigh strain which was worrying him. However, he was reassured and persuaded to play by Jimmy Milne with heavy strapping on his left leg.

North End had that wind at their backs in the first half. It was so prevailing that any kick, place or drop, from Kelly was often reaching Slater on the bounce at the other end. Indeed on one occasion, Yeats hesitated in judging the flight and the ball bounced completely over him, only Slater's frantic late adjustment keeping the name of 'Kelly' off the score sheet!

Preston continued to employ the system of close marking that had so upset Bill Shankly in the two previous encounters. Whenever a Liverpool player received the ball he would have a North Ender harrying him into a hasty pass that was often mistimed or ill judged. Melia, who had proved himself a tireless, hard working midfielder in the Deepdale replay, was subdued by the close attentions of North End defenders cutting off supply lines to Hunt and St John in the process. Whether a supply line would have made any difference to St John is debatable. He could make nothing of proud Prestonian Singleton, who for the third time in ten days, made sure the Scottish international was nothing more than a spectator.

Liverpool didn't seem as front footed in this match, and were struggling to make an impact. Shankly switched the wingers, Callaghan and A'Court around to see if Cunningham and Ross could be breached in any small way, but the full backs were unfazed and remained rock solid.

In a half of few chances of any substance, it was notable that perhaps Liverpool were doubting themselves as to whether they could ever take this tie away from North End. It was they who were beginning to look desperate tactically. One factor that was now a worry for the Preston fans was the wind, which Liverpool would now have the benefit of. North End had failed to capitalise on it and Liverpool could be expected to do better.

Whatever was said to the North End players in the dressing room at half time by Jimmy Milne was smart. For the first 20 minutes of the second half, stiff wind and all, North End almost toyed with Liverpool. They had obviously been told to seize possession at every opportunity and hold the ball. This they did, with great effect; the prolonged spells of brisk but progressive man to man passing completely bewitching Liverpool.

Youngsters Spavin, Wilson and Thompson were excellent. Wilson tantalised the life out of Leishman to the point where the big left half upended the winger and was booked. Spavin linked the Cunningham inspired defence to his midfield domain so smoothly that moves flowed constantly and with ease. Chances started to appear for North End. It could be argued that many should have been converted, but only one was. It finally arrived in the 265th minute of this mammoth contest of attrition.

Half backs, Wylie and Smith moved upfield together exchanging passes. Smith's long ball down the middle was indecisively headed away by Yeats and dropped to Thompson inside the box who drove the goalwards with power past Yeats, catching a slight deflection off Byrne's leg which took it beyond the diving Slater.

North End continued to control the game without too many problems -

Peter Thompson drills home North End's winner against Liverpool

with Liverpool anxiety growing as the clock ticked own. Biggs, unlucky in all three games with various attempts on Slater's goal, grazed the post with a shot then Dawson missed a glorious opportunity.

A superb Wilson cross found Yeats *not* breathing down Dawson's neck for once and with space and time the big centre forward met the ball very powerfully...but directed it wide, with Slater a mere spectator.

There was time for a desperate last ditch Liverpool attack, Kelly grasping Hunt's thunderbolt firmly with less than two minutes left.

At long last the final whistle came. The win obviously meant a lot to captain Willie Cunningham. Beaming from ear to ear he shook hands with all the Liverpool team and officials before trotting down the tunnel. A man happy in his job...

His team had produced a great performance!

7   STALEMATE

.

PRESTON NORTH END 0 MANCHESTER UNITED 0
FA CUP 6TH ROUND 10/3/1962

Having beaten Sheffield Wednesday 2-0 in their fifth round replay at Hillsborough, Manchester United would be North End's quarter final opponents at Deepdale.

There was only one league fixture for North End between finally beating Liverpool and meeting United – a rather dismal home defeat to Stoke City, by 2-1.

Tickets were selling like hot cakes for the United clash. Alas, of the 38,000 tickets printed for the game, some found their way into the ticket touts hands, and they were circling Deepdale looking for prey as kicked off neared. It was reported that £1 stand tickets were selling for between £3 and £4, while a 2/- (10p) Paddock ticket was being hiked up to the princely sum of 12/6 (62.5p)!

Matt Busby had injury concerns before kick off with both David Herd and Albert Quixall failing fitness tests. It meant a reshuffle, so fit again defender Noel Cantwell was handed Herd's shirt, and youngster Phil Chisnall slipped on Quixall's. North End fans would get a glimpse of a certain Nobby Lawton in this game. North End were unchanged:-

Kelly, Cunningham, Ross, Wylie, Singleton, Smith, Wilson, Briggs, Dawson, Spavin and Holden.

The cold weather of the previous few days had abated and the weather was a lot milder but very dull, as the teams ran out to a crescendo of noise. North End kicked off toward the Town End on a very greasy pitch. It was the United defence that was tested first, after the early skirmishes.

Biggs launched a cross field cross into the box which gave Dawson an early chance to challenge David Gaskell in the United goal. Under the sort of aerial pressure that only Dawson could assert, Gaskell dropped the ball just a couple of yards from his goal line. Before Dawson could gather himself, the young keeper had swung around and successfully pouched the ball much to the relief of the United fans that were gathered behind him.

United then thrust forward. In perfection formation and at speed, all five forwards played a part in an attack that resulted in Kelly failing to hold onto a shot; the ball running to Cantwell whose snap shot reply went past the outside of the post.

North End progressed well on one occasion, with Dawson and Spavin swapping passes neatly, but United's defence stood firm - the game was very equal in terms of possession and chances. Wilson was now taking on United's Tony Dunne at every opportunity and proving a real thorn in his side, the left back eventually losing patience and launching himself at the winger. No booking; just a word from the referee and a foul.

For United, Shay Brennan went on a sortie forward before being dispossessed and Jimmy Nicholson hit a great shot on target, only to see it patted down nonchalantly by Kelly.

The first real chance occurred after around 20 minutes. Wilson sped down the wing and delivered a peach of a hard low centre across the face of Gaskell's goal, the ball threading past everybody until it reached Thompson on the opposite side of the box. With United seemingly transfixed, Thompson's shot went inches wide of the near post after beating Gaskell.

United's riposte was swift. In a fast, silky smooth move, the ball was crossed over Kelly and the defence for Nobby Lawton to head back goalwards as North End were on their heels. The header looped accurately towards the top corner, but was snatched out of the air by

Kelly at full stretch.

Bill Foulkes was proving a rock at the heart of the United defence. Many a time he contested a centre with Dawson, and was definitely enjoying a higher success rate than his former colleague. North End however, were confidently holding their own against a classy First Division opposition. The home fans were loud and enthusiastic about their spirited effort.

Cunningham was constantly snapping at heels of Bobby Charlton but the midfielder was a worry as he could obviously spot possible loopholes in the North End back line. Biggs, always looking for the chance to move forward was unlucky when he beat the advancing Gaskell with a shot that clipped the crossbar and went for a goal kick. North End seemed to lift themselves a notch after this and it was Biggs again sweeping in another shot from an inviting pass that had Gaskell clutching on to the ball in the top corner.

Down the field went United, and Charlton drilled a humming low drive that went swerving just by Kelly's post. The pace of the game was becoming frantic, there was no time to dwell on the ball or indeed to consider options for too long. Following a bad Dawson miss – put in the clear eight yards out by Spavin and pushing the ball past keeper and post – United stormed back towards the Kop.

Four times in almost as many seconds did a white shirt block a United attempt as a frantic melee played out; the ball eventually squirting out to Lawton whose shot was finally and gratefully held by Kelly. Charlton then drove a trade mark thunderbolt just wide before the first half ended with Dawson finding the net from a Briggs pass, but from an offside position.

The second half began with Dawson fluffing another golden chance following a perfectly crafted Thompson centre; his sliced shot went agonisingly wide of the post with Gaskell floundering. Half back Smith then ventured forward, and hit a speculative drive at goal. Although it was covered by Gaskell, the ball scraped the outside of the post as it went out of play.

Charlton, Lawton and Cantwell then operated a waspish move that culminated in a grateful Ross taking the chance to decisively punt the ball clear of the impending danger. Cunningham was likewise employed, this time to deny Chisnall.

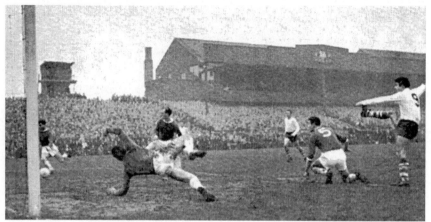

Dawson slices the ball wide with the United defence at sixes and sevens

Charlton was asserting himself now, and treated the crowd to a magnificent piece of play. Cutting in from wide and body swerving at pace past a statuesque Cunningham, he pushed forward a further couple of yards before launching a pile driver at the North End goal from an angle. It looked a goal all the way as the ball left Kelly in its trail, but somehow the covering Ross managed to boot the ball clear off the goal line.

As the half was played out there appeared to be more gaps appearing for the ever prepared United, Johnny Giles spotting an opportunity to test Kelly to the limit with an accurate shot from just outside the box.

Lawton, who had been increasingly frustrating the home fans with his niggling methods towards any North Ender he could get near, was caught in the act by the referee who promptly entered his name into his little black book despite the usual protests.

Spavin, industrious as ever, played in Thompson with the sweetest of passes. It led to a period of intense pressure around the United box, culminating with Briggs driving in a powerful shot that saw Brennan's outstretched leg save United from going a goal behind.

Towards the end of the game, Cunningham was injured when he collided with the onrushing Lawton just inside the North End half. United continued to play on with Preston's senior pro writhing on the ground, the move only ending when the alert Ross cleared with conviction from close to his goal line.

Attention was swung back to midfield, and Cunningham was finally allowed to be assessed. Sadly, after a few minutes, it resulted in the lionhearted Scot being stretchered off the pitch to a huge round of applause from the appreciative North End crowd.

The game ended with neither team in ascendancy. It was back to Old Trafford again for North End, who were hoping that the outcome would be exactly the same as last time!

8   A BRIDGE TOO FAR

MANCHESTER UNITED 2 PRESTON NORTH END 1
FA CUP 6TH ROUND REPLAY 14/3/1962

North End's task was made all the more difficult when it was announced early in the week that Cunningham, the team's inspiration in this FA Cup campaign, would not be taking part.

Still suffering from his collision with Lawton on Saturday, the veteran would have to watch from the sidelines.

It was to be the decisive factor. I imagine it was with some trepidation that stand-in full back Bob Wilson took on the task of man marking Charlton; but he stuck to his task admirably, and gave his best. Otherwise the North End team was unchanged, however the problem North End had with England international Charlton in full flow - on his home ground - cheered on by the United masses - was that it needed some real expertise blocking his way forward. Force him down the line, his pace and strength prevailed. Direct him infield, and the lethal shot on the run from either foot was a constant threat. Every scything Charlton run destabilsed the North End defence a little more.

After about 20 minutes, United embarked on a spell of complete supremacy. Within the next 20 minutes they would score two goals and have two others disallowed.

It was carnage in the North End defence as Charlton beat Wilson.R and swung infield. Singleton hesitated and did not tackle. Charlton immediately launched a low hard drive at the North End goal that Kelly just about caught a fleeting glimpse of as it passed him by. The ball hit the back of the net with the keeper still airborne and United were up and running.

The action and incidents just flowed from then on in this magical United spell. Ross had his name taken for his close attention to Quixall; a header from Herd and a shot from Lawton in quick succession tested Kelly to the full. North End could just not get the ball away.

Lawton stepped over the mark when competing for a loose ball near the goal line with Kelly, bundling both ball and goalkeeper over the line. The referee rightly dismissed Lawton's claim that his challenge was fair.

Lawton then dispossessed Wylie by knocking him to the ground, took the ball forward, rounded Kelly and slotted home. This didn't earn him a goal either, instead just a prolonged finger wagging from the referee.

United were still going for the throat and it was no surprise when Herd inevitably put them further ahead. Flicking the ball to the side of Singleton, the ex Arsenal centre forward met the ball perfectly on its descent, smashing a low volley past the helpless Kelly. The North End fans present must have wondered if a cricket score was on the cards, but the sanctuary of half time break was just a few minutes away and it was hoped that manager Milne could at least hit the 'reset' button.

It seemed as though he may have done so as North End started strongly and went close to nicking a goal back. Dawson hurriedly retrieved the ball after it had gone out of play for a North End throw. Obviously spotting a possibility, he threw the ball in play smartly for Biggs to run on to, leaving United's back line completely flat footed for once.

Biggs took the ball in his stride and hared forward with the defence in pursuit. As he approached the area, Gaskell was on the move narrowing the angle. Biggs pulled the trigger and shot at the gap between keeper and near post. The ball went past Gaskell, but agonisingly just wide of the post.

As the half developed, we were seeing more of North End. Not for the first time in this season's FA Cup exploits, Wilson.D was the stand out performer. A product of that generously talented 1960 North End youth team, he played like a man possessed in the second half. How North End were blessed to have that skilled youth of Thompson and Wilson on the wings!

The United left back Dunne always seemed to be trailing in Wilson's wake; indeed had the referee seen the defenders blatant holding down of the flyer in the area, a penalty would surely have been awarded.

Actually, Wilson very nearly opened the scoring for North End when Wylie pushed a free kick sideways to him. Unleashing a shot that ranked with anything that Charlton or Herd had produced, Gaskell pulled off a spectacular save that just about kept North End at nil.

North End certainly deserved something however, and it arrived mid way through the half. Unsurprisingly, Wilson was involved.

After a barnstorming run down the wing and then cutting in towards the goal, Wilson's superb cross was headed away - anywhere - by Foulkes, desperately back peddling. The ball landed at the feet of Spavin near the edge of the box, who drilled the ball straight back into the net. It was due reward.

North End were missing the punch of Dawson who was totally off his game in this encounter. It was a disappointment to the 5,000 or so North End fans in the crowd and even to some of the home fans who remembered Dawson with some affection. Spavin had taken the bull by the horns and was pushing himself higher up the field to compensate.

Thompson, quiet for the most part, almost put North End on parity with a shot - or was it a teasing centre? - which swirled towards the goal. Gaskell was totally off balance and rather fortunate that the ball went just wide.

Time was petering out as Lawton, (much, much more of him later...), missed a sitter and Charlton shot wide.

A crowd of 63,352 (with another 5,000 locked out when the gates were closed) witnessed the match that saw North End's interest in the competition end for another year. The Lilywhites had acquitted themselves very well in this cup run, and could hold their heads up high.

FINE SHOTS FINISH OFF NORTH END

THEIR defence prised open for the first time after five FA Cup games, North End ceased their interests in Wembley and a weekend in London, by being beaten by 2—1 by Manchester United, in the trophy's sixth round replay at Old Trafford, last

9   LEAVING IT LATE

SOUTHAMPTON 4 PRESTON NORTH END 5
DIVISION TWO   7/9/1963

After leaving one copy of North End's team sheet with the referee, it was a worried looking Jimmy Milne who made his way to the Southampton secretary's office.

He apologised for having to make so many alterations to the team named in the official programme - six in all - but as he explained to any who would listen, *"We are having a terrible time of it with injuries."*

Ian Davidson, Alan Spavin and new signing Alec Ashworth were all out, which forced a raft of positional changes. The team that took the field read like this :-

Kelly, Ross, Donnelly, Kendall, Singleton, Smith, Wilson, Lawton, Dawson, Barber, Holden.

'Saints' were unbeaten at home for the last 21 league games, while North End had made an indifferent start to the season, giving no indication yet as to what a fantastic campaign this would eventually turn out to be.

Both teams had efforts on goal in the opening couple of minutes. Southampton won a corner but Kelly saved Dave Burnside's header with Ease, then Lawton hit a surprise drive on target which the home keeper finally collected after initially only parrying the ball.

Ross, venturing into midfield, was involved in a heavy tackle which must have caused hearts to flutter in the North End dug out when the right back failed to get to his feet straight away. Only the soothing, magical cold water administered by trainer Walter Crook finally enabled Ross to limp away and resume his position.

It was to be expected that North End with so many alterations wouldn't settle so quickly, and this proved to be the case. To their credit however, when in possession they were visibly passing to teammates at every opportunity, giving them a much needed feel of the ball and availing themselves some degree of confidence with each other.

Gradually, a semblance of organisation was filtering through the Preston ranks and they started to take the game forward after the 'induction.' Ross caught the eye with some deft passing when he moved up to support the North End midfield. The ball was played out to Wilson, whose quick cross was a split second too early for Dawson, and the ball ran to safety for the home team.

John Sydenham, very fleet of foot, cut into the North End box, but Singleton just managed to toe end the ball away for a corner before any damage was done. It was the first of three corners in as many minutes as the Southampton upped the ante. The danger was finally over when Saints right half Ken Wimshurst blasted over a full blooded drive. Dawson was begin to bustle about up front, and giving Saints centre half Tony Knapp a lot to think about. He was within a whisker yet again of connecting with a Wilson cross, Knapp having to pick himself up and dust himself down as a result.

Considering North End's mass of late changes and adjustments, they were showing some spirit, looking particularly strong on the right with Ross, Kendall and Wilson all 'performing.' Kendall was particularly industrious; his movement flowed, and he certainly had the ability to spot a possible opening.

Southampton came alive around the half hour mark, when first George O'Brien and then England winger Terry Paine both hit shots that flashed across the face of the North End goal with Kelly beaten.

Another series of scares for North End began when Kelly pushed out a good shot from Sydenham for a corner. The goalkeeper then tipped away an overhead lob from O'Brien before Burnside sent in an header that bounced off the top of the North End crossbar. Hectic was the word as Southampton pushed forward again and went ahead through centre forward George Kirby, who up to that point had been rather anonymous. Sydenham sent in Saints eighth corner from North End's left, and Kirby, snapping into life, hurried forward to meet the centre and nod the ball past Kelly from around six yards out.

All the North End promise of the first half hour seemed to be rapidly dissipating as Southampton went for a second goal. Sloppy defending and a touch of panic were evident, but as so often happens in football, the unbelievable happened.

A few minutes before half time a Wilson shot was tipped over the bar by Reynolds for a North End corner. Meeting the wingers corner well, Dawson jabbed the ball outwards straight into the path of waiting Lawton whose snap shot was belted low through a sea of defenders legs and into the back of the net.

Despite a couple of nervous spells, it was no less than North End deserved with everything taken into consideration. The mug of tea and slice of orange must have tasted so much better as Milne went through his half time notes.

Southampton came out all guns blazing for the second half and Burnside found himself one on one with Kelly just four yards out but incredibly sliced the chance wide with Kelly looking with bemusement for his absent back line. The North End keeper had been the subject of some bashing around in this game, indeed just before the interval Paine had been cautioned by the referee for inflicting a nasty knock when it had seemed easier to pull out of the situation.

He was 'in the wars' again soon after the Burnside miss. Collecting a cross, he was involved in a clash of heads with Kirby - quite innocently - and had to receive prolonged treatment from Walter Crook, who then stood behind the goals for a further five minutes just in case there was a delayed reaction.

On 57 minutes, Sydenham eluded the limpet-like Ross and lofted the ball into the box. Unable to take the ball cleanly, Kelly managed to push the ball away to the edge of the box, but Burnside was waiting and slammed the ball in for Saints second.

Were North End disheartened?

Not a jot, and especially when a thunderous Dawson shot hit the back of the Southampton net just two minutes later. Cue wild North End team celebrations! Moreover, the goal obviously threw a switch on within Dawson and he started rampaging within the Southampton defence like a bull, causing mayhem. He was everywhere Southampton didn't want him to be, and another hard shot from him hit the side netting with Reynolds beaten.

Meanwhile, at the other end, Kelly's legs had turned to jelly, the referee instantly waving on the North End trainer. Again after treating Kelly, he stood beside the goal for a good five minutes to watch for any more lingering after effects.

Kelly wasn't alone. When Dawson and Knapp collided on 70 minutes, the earth shook – Knapp's left foot being badly damaged enough for him to leave the field for attention before returning five minutes later.

It was North End who went very close again when a Smith drive was headed off the line by Williams with Reynolds clawing at air. This was developing into quite a finale, and within a couple of minutes of Kirby missing a scoring opportunity for Saints, Wilson powered down the right wing for North End. Crossing the ball on the run, the centre was superbly met by Dawson, soaring above the Southampton defence and guiding the ball perfectly past Reynolds.

Within three minutes North End were pegged back, Kirby making it 3-3 with just ten minutes left. Sydenham's teasing corner was met by the centre forward and flashed past Kelly before he could react.

It prompted a surrounding of the referee by North End, who obviously thought they had seen an infringement, but the only thing that this achieved was the addition of Tony Barber's name into the referees book.
Three minutes of further to and fro-ing, and then another North End

goal to make it 4-3 to the Lilywhites! And what a goal...

Alex Dawson – rampaged like a bull through the Southampton defence

Collecting the ball near the half way line, Kendall progressed...and progressed further until he was well within the penalty box with defenders in his wake before unleashing a low hard shot that gave Reynolds no chance.

Surely that was it – but no! The excitement was elevated into a frenzy as Southampton equalised with just three minutes left. A shot from Burnside hit the North End crossbar and bounced back into the penalty area; O'Brien lobbing it back into the net before anybody could react. The Dell was rocking. Southampton had come back twice to salvage a point in a superb contest. Or so they thought...

With little more than a minute left, North End went down the field again, and got the ball into the Saints box. With bodies everywhere, the ball fell to Lawton, his first shot – blocked; his second shot – blocked; his third shot – hard, low and buried deep into the back of the net!

What an afternoon and what a performance! It was a sign of things to come in what was going to be by far North End's best season of the Sixties.

10   ROSES CONFRONTATION

LEEDS UNITED 1 PRESTON NORTH END 1
DIVISION TWO   16/11/1963

North End travelled to Elland Road for a top of the table clash against Don Revie's 'on the move' Leeds United feeling rather pleased with themselves.

Unbeaten since October 2nd, they had won five of their last six league games, raking in 11 points from a possible 12. This had placed them firmly amongst the promotion contenders, the other runners besides Leeds United being Sunderland and Charlton Athletic.

Make no mistake, Leeds United *were* on the march. This was the very beginning of their era; 'their time.'

They were somewhat tempestuous league leaders. There is no doubt that they had talented personnel in their team but had gained the reputation of being, 'a win at absolutely all costs' team, quite prepared to resort to the darker side of the game to secure a result.

Even their local press had noticed it, pointing it out with increasing frequency in headlines with such as, *'Warning to Leeds United'* and *'Leeds United Must Calm Down'*.

They were blessed during the 1963/64 season with amongst others, three diminutive and very competitive players in Billy Bremner, Bobby Collins and Johnny Giles. All were superb at their job; and all could spark off a full scale argument with themselves in the confines of a telephone box. Bremner had received a written warning about the number of bookings already accumulated, but Don Revie thought Bremner was more *'sinned against than a sinner.'*

"I have told Bremner to go in hard for the ball in the tackle, which he does. I think he is singled out for punishment by the opposition."

Buoyed by the apparent success of the unforgiving Revie approach of provocation, antagonism and gamesmanship towards both opposition and referee, they carried on regardless.

The team news announced on Friday was that Leeds' leading scorer, Don Weston would miss out due to a thigh strain, but would be replaced by the more than useful Jim Storrie. North End would be without Alec Ashworth, giving new recruit Brian Godfrey another chance to shine alongside Alex Dawson.

A crowd of over 33,000 was in the ground as the teams entered the arena.

North End fielded :-

Kelly, Ross, Smith, Lawton, Singleton, Davidson, Wilson, Godfrey, Dawson, Spavin, Holden.

As Leeds were in all white, North End were in royal blue shirts and white shorts.

Leeds were soon on the front foot asserting themselves. Giles cut inside and the crowd roared as the electric pace of winger Albert Johansen was brought in to play. The resulting centre was cleared by Smith, but returned with interest by Giles, Smith again coming to the rescue to divert the ball away for a corner. North End finally moved upfield, Lawton feeding Dawson with a through ball, but Leeds obviously knew all about the big target man and he was receiving close attention.

Despite this, Dawson got the ball away to Spavin, who then brought Holden into play before the move broke down. Nerves seemed to be playing a part as possession was being surrendered by both teams preventing any sustained pattern of play to develop.

Johansen was lighting up the dull play whenever he received the ball. He obviously had a license to roam, and was indeed turning up everywhere. With his pace and trickiness he was proving to be something of a handful.

Meanwhile Lawton was working extremely hard trying to get North End upfield, but frustratingly the forward line couldn't keep hold of the ball once presented with it.

Johansen then put on the after-burners and went past Ross, but instead of crossing the ball for the waiting posse of attackers, he chose to shoot. Groans of disappointment were audible from the home fans as Kelly collected with ease. Singleton and Davidson were noticeably vigorous with their tackling and clearances and still, despite the best scheming efforts of Lawton and Spavin, nothing was happening up front for North End.

Storrie, just inside the penalty area, passed backwards for Paul Reaney to put in a cross. Storrie flicked the ball onto Ian Lawson, whose shot - executed as he was leaning backwards - banged into the North End crossbar before being hustled to safety. Gary Sprake, a virtual spectator for the first 40 minutes, then gathered in a cross from Holden and fell to the ground, somehow colliding with Dawson. As the keeper received attention, Dawson was given a lecture by the referee.

North End had competed well, until they tried to involve the forwards. They were completely misfiring – unlike the defence, which refused to be bullied and was as doggedly determined and as unyielding as their hosts. A penalty claim was waved away by the referee when Collins went down in the North End box right on half time. A few seconds later, the whistle blew again, this time for the break, where it was hoped the Preston forwards could be given a talking to by Jimmy Milne.

As North End trotted out after the break, Dawson's right hand appeared heavily bandaged.

Within a minute of the restart, the pattern had been set for the rest of the game. Bremner unceremoniously hacked down Lawton to the cheers of the partisan home crowd and was spoken to at length by the referee.

Nothing resulted from the free kick, but shortly afterwards Spavin was left writhing in pain after another dreadful tackle from Bremner - who received yet another lecture from the referee.

Whatever the half time talk was about in the Leeds dressing room, it had certainly widened and brightened the eyes of the home side. Tackling with undue vigour and tenacity, they had obviously been reminded that North End were a serious rival and had to be seen off.

Despite the referee's lectures, the bad feeling on the pitch worsened. Tackles were now flying in from both sides, and a Leeds player had to be restrained from rushing at Singleton. At that point, the referee stopped the game, and called all the players together to give them a finger wagging that lasted almost three minutes.

Yorkshire Post Newspapers
The referee directs both Leeds and North End players to 'cool it'

It was exactly the right course of action. The situation had come to a head largely as a result of North End having to defend themselves from the increased physicality of their hosts play in the second half. The home crowd didn't think so however, roundly booing the referee during his speech to the players.

Soon after the resumption, Lawson made his way into the North End box and fell to the floor as two defenders converged on him. A penalty was awarded, North End arguing vehemently with the referee that the tackle was fair. Finger wagging 'conversation' about the decision continued between the two teams as Collins lined up the spot kick. Into the net it went, the irate home crowd hushed for a while at least as they devoured their pound of flesh.

Leeds maintained their aggressive approach and the North End defence was stretched for a while coping with the frenzied attackers. They held firm, but had every excuse to be rattled with the attack unable to give them any respite or recovery time by at least holding the ball up. As the game entered its final stretch the contest was becoming increasingly one sided, taking part exclusively in the North End half.

Then, quite out of the blue, the wind of change started to blow across Elland Road.

Wilson sprung into life, and cutting in was crudely body checked inches outside of the penalty area. The free kick came to naught, but shortly afterwards Godfrey had a sniff of a chance too but was too slow to pivot and shoot; Sprake easily claiming the mishit ball.

Lawton then cleverly engineered some room and moved forward down the left. He put in a fine cross, which found Holden unmarked. Controlling and shooting the ball for the far corner in an instant, Holden forced Sprake to make the save of the day. Then a minute later following a Wilson corner, Sprake dropped the ball before recovering the situation quickly as the North End forwards moved in.

It was astounding how the flow of the game had changed but Leeds eventually retaliated – and how. Collins carefully placed a free kick from some 35 yards out which swerved and caught the North End crossbar before being cleared.

North End broke away again, and Wilson spotted Smith moving forward and duly crossed the ball; the wing half meeting it well, but heading just wide.

With just under three minutes left, North End left their parting gift.

Somehow Holden got himself involved in some leisurely Leeds play at the back and managed to deflect the ball into the home net after it hit him in the face - to the absolute delight of his teammates. It was a great point gleaned by North End who had refused to be intimidated as so many other teams had been, and indeed would be in the future, by the

Leeds United confrontational style.

The return fixture, at Deepdale later in the season was to be even better!

11 WE WISH YOU A MERRY CHRISTMAS...

CARDIFF CITY 0 PRESTON NORTH END 4
DIVISION TWO 26/12/1963

If ever there was a time to make a watertight case to safeguard the unique English Boxing Day football tradition for ever, it was in 1963.

It's worth giving those results (next page) a good look. The top two tiers produced 104 goals from just 20 fixtures, with North End happy to provide four of them.

There were geographically closer teams to Cardiff than North End that could have rolled into Ninian Park, but the fixtures panel, (no computers to blame in 1963), had to be obeyed! It was in fact a double-header; Cardiff would appear at Deepdale just two days later on Saturday, 28th December for the return fixture.

North End stood a proud third in Division Two, four points behind leaders Leeds United, and just one behind Sunderland with a game in hand on the Mackems.

North End fielded for the sixth time in succession :-

Kelly, Ross, Smith, Lawton, Singleton, Davidson, Wilson, Ashworth, Dawson, Spavin, Holden.

Quite simply, this was an occasion when North End demonstrated their right to be considered promotion candidates.

FOOTBALL LEAGUE DIVISION 1

BLACKPOOL	1-5	CHELSEA
BURNLEY	6-1	MANCHESTER UTD
FULHAM	10-1	IPSWICH TOWN
LEICESTER CITY	2-0	EVERTON
LIVERPOOL	6-1	STOKE CITY
NOTTINGHAM F	3-3	SHEFFIELD UTD
SHEFFIELD WED	3-0	BOLTON WANDERERS
WEST BROMWICH A	4-4	TOTTENHAM H
WEST HAM UTD	2-8	BLACKBURN ROVERS
WOLVERHAMPTON W	3-3	ASTON VILLA

FOOTBALL LEAGUE DIVISION 2

CARDIFF CITY	0-4	PRESTON NORTH END
GRIMSBY TOWN	1-1	LEYTON ORIENT
LEEDS UNITED	1-1	SUNDERLAND
MANCHESTER CITY	8-1	SCUNTHORPE UTD
MIDDLESBROUGH	3-0	DERBY COUNTY
NEWCASTLE UTD	2-0	HUDDERSFIELD T
NORTHAMPTON T	1-3	ROTHERHAM UTD
NORWICH CITY	3-2	SWINDON TOWN
SOUTHAMPTON	1-2	PLYMOUTH ARGYLE
SWANSEA TOWN	1-3	CHARLTON ATHLETIC

Boxing Day results 1963. Goals went in everywhere!

The Ninian Park pitch was far from welcoming. The blanket of snow that had led on the pitch had thawed over the previous couple of days, leaving large and fairly random patches of standing water for the players to contend with.

Milne prepared his team well. Normally an eye catching passing team, he changed the tactics for this encounter - his charges swinging the ball about with longer passes to combat the conditions.

Cardiff City, not as well advised or prepared were therefore on the back foot from the start. It wasn't long before North End went ahead ... just three minutes in fact. City's young full back Peter Rodrigues, wasn't destined to have a *'great day.'* That was reserved for Wilson (see below) who gave Cardiff's U23 international full back - regarded as their discovery of the season - a nightmare of a game.

Wilson has great day

By A SPECIAL CORRESPONDENT

FROM the third minute when David Wilson swept through to score the first of his three goals, there was never any doubting North End's superiority at Ninian Park. Not only did they gain ample revenge for Cardiff's 6—2 win at Deepdale last season, but they produced a brand of football which, if maintained, must keep them strong promotion challengers.

While Preston's main strength lay in the thrust and skill of wing halves Davidson and Lawton, they owed a great deal to the inspiring leadership of Dawson, who time and again cut through to tangle the Welsh

Omen?

Preston North End's 4-0 Yuletide win at Cardiff could be a promotion omen (writes Walter Pilkington).

When last promoted from Division II. as 1950-51 champions, they gained a Christmas Day away win by 4-1 against Queen's, Park Rangers.

It made their points total 22 from 24 matches compared with 34 from 24 games this season.

It was a Rodrigues mistake that started the goal rush. Davidson dispossessed the youngster as he attempted to dribble clear of danger on the treacherous surface. The ball was fed to Wilson who instantly drove the ball home past the helpless Graham Vearncombe in Cardiff's goal.

With Davidson, Spavin and Lawton in complete control of midfield, the

North End forward line was rampant.

While Wilson was undoubtedly the star, Dawson's intelligent running and prompting was proving far too much for the home defence to cope with. Both Dawson and Spavin had hit the bar before left half Davidson strode through the City back line to put North End two up on 38 minutes.

After the half time break, Cardiff desperately tried to lift their game, but anything that they brought to the table was instantly consumed by Ross, Smith and Singleton. With North End finishing as strongly as they started, it was fitting reward for the outstanding Wilson that his quickfire twin salvo of goals in the 75th and 76th minutes gave him the hat trick his performance so richly deserved.

By Saturday morning though, the North End fans were choking on their cornflakes!

N.E. deny £60,000 bid for Wilson

By WALTER PILKINGTON

A BANNER-HEADLINED morning newspaper report that Newcastle Utd have offered £60,000 for Preston North End's outside right David Wilson " to step past Wolves in the race to sign the England Under-23 winger." today was categorically denied at Deepdale.

"No approach, much less a bid, has been made" said manager Jimmy Milne.

A national newspaper ran a story suggesting, with a very prominent headline, that £60,000 had been offered to Preston by Newcastle United for David Wilson, with Wolves still debating whether or not to table a bid of their own.

North End, and in particular Jimmy Milne, dismissed the story straight away, citing the article as, "purely paper talk," adding the story was entirely down to the fact the winger had been the stand-out performer in the Boxing Day dismantling of Cardiff City. "No approach, much less a bid, has been made," the North End manager protested. "These stories can unsettle a player."

Wilson was, however, having a fantastic season. It would have come as no surprise if this story actually did have some substance to it. A quick reference to the online inflation calculator reveals that David Wilson was valued at the equivalent of £1.15M in 1963, by whoever penned the article ... or indeed by Newcastle United ...

12   ...AND A HAPPY NEW YEAR!

PRESTON NORTH END 4 CARDIFF CITY 0
DIVISION TWO   28/12/1963

The Christmas holiday return match at Deepdale against Cardiff City, saw the visitors make four changes.

Out went goalkeeper Graham Vearncombe, along with Ivor Allchurch who had picked up an injury and Peter Rodrigues, after his roasting by Wilson, was omitted. Mel Charles had gone down with 'flu which, fortunately for the Bluebirds, hadn't yet spread to his brother John, who would lead the City attack.

North End were unchanged yet again :-

Kelly, Ross, Smith, Lawton, Singleton, Davidson, Wilson, Ashworth, Dawson, Spavin, Holden

On a fine, mild and bright day North End kicked off towards the Kop.

The early running was made by North End, Ashworth heading over from a Wilson cross. The big striker returned the compliment soon after, advancing Wilson down the right; the resulting corner saved by Dilwyn John in the Cardiff goal.

A few minutes later, another North End corner was only partially cleared by a clutch of City defenders massing in front of John, as though protecting him from Dawson and Ashworth. The ball was cleared only as far as the edge of the area, where it was met by the right boot of the ever alert Ross, whose low drive was eventually held by the goalkeeper.

Cardiff were concentrating on defence, and one or two of their players weren't too fussy either about how they went about it. Following the drubbing North End meted out to them on Boxing Day, they had arrived with a plan which involved clinging like limpets to the home forwards. Dawson, Ashworth, Holden and Wilson all had a shadow.

Wilson was the first to break free. Decisively moving forward, he delivered a pass infield for Ashworth to run onto and strike at goal with some degree of venom, John once again relieved to take possession at the second attempt.

North End eventually took the lead on 24 minutes.

Spavin, weaving his way forward, spotted Lawton around 25 yards out and found him with a neat pass. Quite unexpectedly, Lawton looked up and instantly launched a right foot shot at goal. Rising in classic fashion as it sped towards the angle of post and crossbar, it flew past the outstretched John and into the back of the net. North End were on their way.

Wilson and Ashworth were beginning to link up dangerously now the shackles had been cast off. Trevor Edwards, just like Rodrigues on Boxing Day, was finding Wilson hard to contain. However, despite North End making all the running, Cardiff were happy to spoil the game and break, leaving their hosts vulnerable to a goal against the run of play. So, it was with some relief that after 40 minutes North End put some daylight between the teams, by going two up.

Ashworth bustled through the defence and was unlucky with a shot; the ball hurriedly cleared. Back came Preston, and a cross was superbly met by Dawson, the goal bound header being desperately deflected away by a defender – but only straight into the path of Spavin, who nipped in to gleefully nod the ball home.

Just three minutes later, North End put the game out of reach of Cardiff. They were awarded a penalty for considering what the referee had let go beforehand in the first half, was an innocuous looking challenge.

Bursting into the box, Ashworth was met by Alec Milne and Colin Baker and fell down as Cardiff pair hustled him. Without hesitation, the referee pointed to the spot and Dawson lined up his target as the defenders had their protests waved away.

Dawson didn't mess around with penalties. True to form, this particular cannonball, launched right footed, flashed past the keeper in true *'Black Prince'* tradition.

After just three minutes of second half meanderings, the referee awarded another penalty – but this time to Cardiff.

If Ashworth's award had been soft, this was even less plausible. With the ball bouncing away harmlessly out of the box, it struck Singleton on the forearm when unchallenged and nowhere near goal. This however was enough to convince the referee it was 'intentional' and he instantly pointed to the spot.

Edwards was nominated to take the penalty ... and must have wished he was somewhere else. He drilled a low shot wide of the post, and walked away shaking his head and wishing the ground would open up and swallow him.

North End's response was a series of rousing attacks that stretched Cardiff one way, then the other. Ashworth lashed in a great drive, then soon after Ross drilled a shot in as the ball ran free from the Cardiff box. A second Ashworth penalty claim, the most viable of the afternoon, was instantly waved away by the referee who was stood over the incident.

The visitor's attack was aimless. In the very rare times they managed to cross the half way line they were now being repelled with ease, with Singleton completely dominating John Charles. In fact Cardiff City were woeful.

Before the game drew to a close, the festive crowd of over 16,000 witnessed Ashworth and Dawson combine to smash a way open down the middle, the interplay between the two culminating in Dawson firing a shot home from close range that almost took the net off its hooks. It was his 23rd goal of the season to date – and it still wasn't quite January! North End had plundered eight goals without reply in 180 minutes against the Welshmen; nobody could have asked for more.

Division Two – December 28th 1963

		P	W	D	L	F	A	PTS
1	Leeds United	25	14	9	2	42	19	37
2	Sunderland	26	15	6	5	45	28	36
3	**Preston North End**	25	14	8	3	52	33	36

Certainly this was a happy Christmas for all North End fans ... and there was much more to come in the new year!

13   RUN RAGGED

PRESTON NORTH END 2 LEEDS UNITED 0
DIVISION TWO   3/3/1964

By now, North End had embarked on their 1964 FA Cup adventure; however this particular and very crucial league game took place just a few days after the sixth round success at Oxford United - more of the FA Cup later.

With the 'Cup' now much more than a pleasant distraction, North End were not falling into the trap of tailing off in the league - just yet anyway - as they still harboured genuine promotion ambitions.

This was a genuine 'four-pointer.' Win, and North End were level second with Leeds United on both games and points; lose, and they would be four points behind the Yorkshiremen with the same amount of games played. Preston just *had* to win!

For those present at the game, few will have seen a more stirring display from any North End team. It was unforgettable.

A crowd of 35,612 packed into Deepdale to witness this fast paced, crackerjack of a game. The appointment of Jim Finney as referee was probably due to the shenanigans that occurred at Elland Road earlier in the season between the two teams. Finney was regarded as one of England's top referees.

Within the first couple of minutes, with the crowd decibels unbearable, North End had forced two corners and Leeds United one. Play was fast and furious, and it needed the calming presence of Mr. Finney to stamp out the niggles that inevitably followed.

He was forced to book Willie Bell, the Leeds United left back for an awful challenge on Wilson after already lecturing him for an overzealous challenge on Holden. Bobby Collins was then spoken to for a challenge on Lawton that left the North End captain on the floor, before Dawson hurled himself illegally at Gary Sprake in a challenge for a high ball.

Disappointingly, the Leeds 'style' had not changed since the last meeting with North End, but as in the previous encounter, North End were not going to be bullied.

Ashworth found himself in space and with the ball invitingly played in front of him by Lawton, crashed in a powerful drive that Sprake did well to hold onto.

There was a real battle for supremacy going on in midfield. With the referee on top of the play, the footballing skills of captains Lawton and Collins were shining through for all to see.

The speed and danger of Albert Johansen was being well nullified by Ross, who patently refused to allow the flyer down the line. Repeatedly forced inside he was nowhere near as effective, possession often being lost to North End's midfield.

End to end the battle became, as Leeds came close to Kelly's goal the high pitched screams of anxiety from some the home crowd could be heard over the held breaths of the majority. One such incident - when Lawton toe poked the ball away for a corner from Alan Peacock as he was about to shoot, almost led to Leeds opening the scoring. The corner was swung in and Jim Storrie found himself in acres of space, only to fluff the chance by blasting high and wide.

That 'terror' turned to joy however, within seconds.

Holden, speeding down the left wing, cut in and played a perfect ball for Dawson to run onto. The 'Black Prince' duly launched the cannonball so powerfully that Sprake couldn't hold it, pushing it to his right. Before the ball could run over the line for a corner, Ashworth nipped in and deftly tapped the ball into the net from the oblique angle. The noise was deafening. It was a fully deserved reward for all North End's endeavours.

If anything, this had the effect of lifting the game's tempo even more. Incidents at both ends continued apace – Jack Charlton could, and should, have equalised but could not control his close range shot under pressure. He then appeared to handle the ball in the Leeds penalty area; Mr. Finney waving away Dawson's loud protests.

If that refereeing decision didn't go North End's way, they were breathing a huge sigh of relief when the next one did. Following an almighty goalmouth scramble in the North End box, Storrie had the ball in the net, but before he could celebrate, Mr. Finney, blew loud and shrill on his whistle for handball.

Half time finally arrived and the teams trooped off for a brew and their tactical talks with loud applause ringing in their ears.

After the restart, a Grenville Hair free kick saw Peacock go close after getting the better of Singleton for once, but Kelly was on hand to calm things down with an easy save. Then 12 minutes into the second half, Wilson settled Leeds fate.

It came from nowhere. Moving in from the wing he worked his way to the middle, whereupon he unleashed a sudden left foot shot from all of 25 yards out. Dipping noticeably as it flew into the top corner of the net, it left Sprake rooted to the ground.

There followed scenes of great jubilation. While Wilson was celebrating by running around like a gazelle, the Leeds players were just looking at each other in bewilderment. There had appeared to be no danger; they had been taken completely by surprise by Wilson's glorious strike.

North End now turned the screw. There was to be no relaxation of the grip they now had on this game and they drove forward with speed and venom at every opportunity. Spavin and Davidson emerged to dominate the middle of the field with Lawton, and Leeds were beginning to feel the pinch. The pressure was relentlessly sustained.

Driving down the wings to deafening noise, Holden and Wilson constantly had Bell and Hair back pedaling along with the rest of the Leeds defence as they frequently brought Dawson and Ashworth into play. This unremitting roasting saw Norman Hunter amongst others bent double gasping for respite at one point when the ball went out of play.

This was indisputably the definition of *'running a team ragged.'*

Leeds were not promotion favourites for nothing however, and with about 15 minutes left they gave it one last go. First, Johnny Giles grazed the crossbar with a snap shot, then both Bell and Collins shot over when they should have done better. At the other end Ashworth was within inches of scoring North End's third when Wilson sent a low centre arrowing across the face of the Leeds' goal.

With fingernails down to the quick, and the fans anxiously counting down the minutes, the match was finally brought to a close. Preston North End stood joint second in the Division Two and were in the FA Cup Semi Finals. What a season this was!

North End skipper Nobby Lawton later reflected,

"Two months before the '64 final we had played Leeds at Deepdale. They won the Second Division title that season, with Giles, Hunter, Bremner and Charlton in their side.
"It was the beginning of that great Leeds era, but we destroyed them at Deepdale 2-0.
"Leeds never got a kick, and that night I realised we were a great team. We played so well against Leeds I didn't want it to end."

14   COLD COMFORT

PRESTON NORTH END 1 NOTTINGHAM FOREST 0
FA CUP 3RD ROUND REPLAY 13/1/1964

Lots of memorable sporting events occurred in 1964.

Cassius Clay fought Sonny Liston for Boxing's heavyweight title, Fred Trueman took his 300th Test wicket, the Tokyo Olympic Games were held, Arkle won the Cheltenham Gold Cup, Match of the Day was launched on the new BBC2, and North End began their FA Cup journey!

It's fair to say that if you are a fan of any team that reaches the FA Cup Final, especially when you aren't really expected to, then every step along the road to Wembley is 'memorable' in some way or other.

North End began their FA Cup journey of 1964 by being drawn away to Nottingham Forest, a team sat comfortably in 13th position of Division One, well clear of any relegation issues, just nine points behind the leaders.

A crowd of over 26,000 had witnessed the teams run out at the City Ground on 4th January to the sound of Britain's foremost pop group of the time, The Beatles, pounding out their latest No.1 'I Want To Hold Your Hand' over the tannoy.

It turned out to be a game with some degree of stalemate attached, but at the same time very heartening that North End could hold their own against such an established Division One team.

The country was in the grip of a quite severe winter and any plans for the replay that was penciled in for Tuesday, January 7th had to be scrapped. Instead the game took place the following Monday - in continuous snowfall - but was well worth waiting for.

Smith was carrying an injury and left out of the re-arranged North End team for the replay, the Lilywhites lining up with:-

Kelly, Ross, Davidson, Lawton, Singleton, Kendall, Wilson, Ashworth, Dawson, Spavin, Holden.

Howard Kendall had by that time played a few games for the North End first team, so could be expected to slot in well on his latest tour of duty.

With North End going well in the league, a crowd of 29,324 spectators turned up to cheer them on. The game set off at a frantic pace, with North End dominant.

The pitch, constantly refreshed by the persistent snow was keeping the surface slippery and making life difficult for the players. Indeed, the by-lines were swept a few times too during the game to keep them visible.

Ashworth was making a nuisance of himself, but Forest were very well organised in defence and were quite content to draw North End's sting.

Peter Grummitt in the Forest goal looked strikingly good. Very adept at handling the menacing crosses from Holden and Wilson - and anybody else - he gave the impression that he was unbeatable.

Forest began to settle and move the ball around, whilst keeping North End at arm's length. Bob McKinlay and England U23 cap Jeff Whitefoot in particular were tackling well, continually shepherding North End away from their box.

Try as they would, North End could not breach the visitors' resilient barrier, but conversely North End were not being overrun either. Forest's attack had been even quieter than North End's, with Singleton marshalling his defence well.

The competitive football on display was top class, but it was a 'defences on top' type of game.

The second half began, and it was much the same. North End drove forward whenever they could but found the redoubtable Grummitt waiting there for them.

A Spavin run and drive looked every inch a goal until Grummitt's contorted body palmed the ball away - even drawing applause from Spavin himself. Holden then cut in and seemed certain to score...until the airborne Grummitt managed to deflect the shot over the bar.

North End were increasingly attacking, but with Dawson being able to make nothing of McKinlay their options were somewhat diminished.

This enthralling game just lacked a goal. The two teams were gamely contesting proceedings in poor conditions but the shivering, snow covered crowd were now asked to stay at Deepdale for a further half hour as the whistle blew with the teams level on 90 minutes.

The two managers, Jimmy Milne and Johnny Carey made their way onto the pitch to speak to their teams. North End listened intently to Milne, with heads bowed, and ran away sprightly to their starting positions.

What followed was a glorious half hour of football from North End. Lifting the tempo of the match to its limit, they set about Forest, determined to come away with the spoils.

The Forest defenders, so accomplished during the 90 minutes just passed, were rattled by the immediate ferocity of the North End raids and started to display a degree of panic and vulnerability.

Three minutes into extra time the ball was repelled to just beyond the confines of the Forest penalty area with a hint of desperation as Dawson marauded in front of the visitors' goal.

Before the defenders could blink, Kendall ran onto the loose ball and launched a rocket shot that the hitherto invincible Grummitt could not

North End triumph in Cup

thriller

Dynamic decider by Kendall

By WALTER PILKINGTON

PRESTON NORTH END are through to the fourth round of the FA Cup. They will visit Bolton Wanderers on Saturday week, and the home side's resolute approach to their task in last night's post-

poned replay with Nottingham Forest at Deepdale left no doubt that they fully realised the prize was worth the extra effort.

I rate their eventual mastery of a First Division team, robbed of . . . its . . . comparative . . .

As soon that suggestions had begun, North End sought to storm a way through immediately extra time started and the ferocity of their attacks proved . . . the Forest rearguard.

The ball was running during the replay hut . . . Kendall . . . Dynamically, to apply the final thrust . . . to just beyond the penalty area. Before the goalkeeper had time to collect their senses, the Kendall . . .

The goal that sunk Nottingham Forest. Kendall's rocket shot leaves Grummitt pawing the air

69

save, vainly waving goodbye to it as it flew by.

There was bedlam as both the North End crowd and players celebrated, their tensions simultaneously released. Dawson grabbed the youngster and lifted him aloft joyously for all to spectators to see.

It was a great moment for Kendall who had slotted seamlessly into the first team when in fact he should have been appearing for the North End FA Youth Cup team at Maine Road against Manchester City.

The revitalised North End continued to dominate from midfield, and as time ticked by it looked as though the taking of that one half chance by Kendall was going to put North End on the bus to Bolton for the fourth round. It so nearly wasn't the case though.

Forest winger Ian Storey-Moore - another star of the future - was put through but made a complete hash of his attempt on goal. However, Kelly didn't save cleanly, and with Storey-Moore sensing he could make amends, it was the reassuring right boot of Singleton through the ball that saw off the danger.

Lawton had an inspirational game in the middle of the field, ensuring North End's brand of wholehearted and intelligent play won the day. Spavin, Holden and Ross were all stand-outs and Singleton was like a rock in the centre of defence.

It was quite an achievement to draw away and defeat at home a more than average Division One team in the FA Cup, and encouragingly demonstrated that North End could possibly hold their own in the top flight, should they achieve their parallel 1964 football dream of promotion from Division Two.

15   A BRILLIANT BRACE

BOLTON WANDERERS 2 PRESTON NORTH END 2
FA CUP 4TH ROUND 25/1/1964

With North End facing first division opponents one again, interest was massive for this all-Lancashire tie with North End quickly swiftly shifting their full 10,000 quota of tickets.

In fact on the big day, with all roads leading to the ground being completely blocked, the two coaches carrying the North End team and officials had to be afforded a police escort.

Smith's leg injury had still not mended, and Ashworth had developed a thigh strain, so North End fielded:-

Kelly, Ross, Davidson, Lawton, Singleton, Kendall, Wilson, Godfrey, Dawson, Spavin, Holden.

It was a mild but dull day as 'captain for the day' Holden led out North End on his first return to his old club since his move to Deepdale. Approaching 40,000 fans where shoehorned into Burnden Park and the noise upon the teams' arrival was deafening.

Both teams were wearing their change kits. Bolton in their red shirts and white shorts, North End in royal blue shirts and white shorts.

The early exchanges were very exploratory. As the crowd bellowed from the sides, the players were summing each other up finding their feet in what was to be a classic contest.

The first sortie to demonstrate any type of threat was made by North End, when linkman Spavin looked up and fired in a spontaneous 20 yard drive at the Bolton goal, which Eddie Hopkinson followed and patted down with ease.

Play continued at a fast pace but North End's close, tight marking was having the desired subduing effect on the home side. They weren't making much headway and it was the brighter football of North End that put Lawton into a good position; his shot not held cleanly by Hopkinson and trickling towards the goal line before the keepers second grab made the situation safe.

This had the affect of rousing Bolton, and they finally launched a few raids of their own, the best of which saw winger Gordon Taylor hit a snap shot that Kelly had to palm over his crossbar. Taylor was looking impressive and a real handful for full back Ross, who was being tested to the limit.

The game was warming up nicely now and North End combined well to put Dawson in the clear. The footballing 'colossus' (definition *: a person or thing of enormous size, importance, or ability*) lashed his shot at goal but it struck the base of the post, glancing away to safety. At the other end, Bolton centre forward Wyn Davies broke clear and tested Kelly with a fine shot that he deflected for a corner.

Back down the field came the visitors, Spavin scheming and prompting, tried another long range shot that forced Hopkinson to punch well clear, the ball then being nicely worked forward by the home team. This promising attack came to nothing as the North End defence was asserting itself well by now, looking solid with no visible loopholes.

Lawton was at his best. Organising, demanding and driving his team forward at every opportunity. It was he who passed to Wilson who, with deft footwork, created an opening that saw his 15 yard shot saved by Hopkinson. Relative newcomer to the North End club, Godfrey, had been working hard and he tried his luck with a good shot that the ever vigilant Hopkinson covered well.

North End were certainly looking more polished than their Division One hosts, who didn't seem to have the same creativity or slickness about their play.

Francis Lee, who had been held in check for the majority of the first half by Davidson finally broke free of his shackles and ran clear of the left back. Giving Kendall the slip along the way, he passed to Freddie Hill whose shot at goal was saved well by Kelly.

Kelly then needed prolonged treatment to his shoulder, as when picking up a back pass, Davis barged into him in true Lofthouse tradition, laying him out flat.

This signaled a resurgence of sorts from the Bolton attack who thought that strong arm tactics were the way to progress. Preston's defence stood their ground however, and the game eventually returned to its previous default of the visitors looking the more likely team.

A period of North End pressure finally brought due reward for their mastery in the 35th minute. Godfrey from wide left, delivered a centre that was hit as hard as a shot. Dawson, sensing this was the chance to end what for him had been a barren spell in front of goal, hurtled forward then fearlessly leapt high to meet it. The ball was headed with such speed and unerring accuracy that Hopkinson hardly moved before picking the ball out of the net.

What a goal and what a noise from the appreciative North End contingent in the crowd!

In the run up to half time, Lee could well have equalised for Bolton with a better directed header and at the other end, good shots from both Wilson and Holden were dealt with by Hopkinson.

North End retreated to the dressing room for their refreshments to tremendous cheers from their fans. They had looked polished, unflappable and destined for the fifth round.

Hopkinson was soon in action after the restart, smartly dealing with crosses from both wings aimed at Dawson. The Bolton keeper had looked in every way the England international he once was, demonstrating goalkeeping at his efficient best. Play broke towards the North End goal and when Hill slipped a through ball in for Taylor to run

Dawson's Double

Top – Dawson buries Godfrey's cross past Hopkinson to open the scoring for
North End in the FA Cup tie at Burnden Park

Bottom – Dawson leaps high to head home powerfully into the roof of the
Bolton Wanderers net to put North End 2-0 in front

onto it looked like the winger would be one on one with Kelly, but Ross showing speed of thought had anticipated the situation well, calmly shepherding the ball back to his keeper.

Indeed it was the redoubtable Ross using his initiative, who set things up for Dawson to score his, and North End's second in the 66th minute. Well forward, and seeing the potential of Dawson's movement, the full back crossed the ball perfectly for him to have a short dart at with some purpose. Leaping high above the challenging Bryan Edwards, the impact was perfect and the ball superbly directed like a bullet into the roof of the net. Hopkinson was rooted to the ground like an ancient oak.

Sheer, sheer brilliance all round, and once more the North End fans made a massive din. Seemingly now in control and the fifth round just 22 minutes away, North End were suddenly rocked.

Bolton inside left, Peter Deakin lined up a free kick from all of 20 yards out. Somehow, his hard low drive found a gap in the North End wall, and carried on its slanted approach evading Kelly and duly finding the corner of the net.

Fortified by this and with the home crowd now urging Bolton forward, North End were backpedaling. Bolton certainly had the bit between their teeth and all the action was in the vicinity of the visitors box. This renewed drive acheived its purpose after 74 minutes when Deakin equalised. Taylor drilled the ball in from the left into the crowded box where it bobbed around before the inside forward poked the ball past Kelly's despairing dive.

Further damage was avoided, and North End were back in some sort of control by the time the final whistle blew.

What a great cup tie it had been, and more of the same to look forward to in the replay at Deepdale. Fantastic, fantastic Preston North End!

16   FRANTIC FOOTBALL

PRESTON NORTH END 2 BOLTON WANDERERS 1
FA CUP 4TH ROUND REPLAY 27/1/1964

You had to admire the efficiency. Directly underneath the match report in the previous Saturday's *'Last Football'* newspaper were detailed instructions about the match ticket arrangements for the Deepdale replay along with a Ribble Buses message about the 'pick up' times for fans living in the surrounding areas of Preston. Match tickets were only necessary to gain access to the stands, the rest of the ground was pay at the turnstile.

Monday night couldn't come around quick enough. North End were in with a great chance of adding another Division One scalp to their 1964 collection. There was another bonus too. Following the lunchtime draw for the fifth round, the prospect of playing Carlisle United from Division Four - and maybe a smooth path to the quarter finals - meant that 38,290 very attracted fans crammed into Deepdale, wisely deciding to forego the latest episode of *Coronation Street*...

The noise was deafening as the unchanged teams ran out. Both clubs had decided to retain their secondary strips as worn in the game at Burnden Park.

Whether it was adrenalin pumping or just the will to knock over the local opposition, the game set off at an unbelievably frantic pace.

North End seemed to be under instructions to 'shoot on sight' wherever possible, as shots from Holden, Wilson and Spavin demanded total concentration from Eddie Hopkinson in the Bolton goal.

Lawton and Spavin were soon at ease in midfield, the latter in particular stroking passes to each flank with time and precision amongst the general on-field bedlam.

North End didn't monopolise the attacking play however, with Bolton making the home crowd squirm with a hard low shot from Francis Lee and a long range effort from Freddie Hill, both of which brought good saves from Kelly.

For any defender around that time, the huge figure of Dawson running rampantly at them with the ball was the very last that they would have chosen.

This however was the dilemma facing Bryan Edwards, the visitors centre half. His attempted tackle saw him bounce off the centre forward rather in the fashion of snow being shunted aside by a huge plough.

There was no question of falling to the ground and rolling around as in these current days of non-contact play and amateur dramatics; Dawson simply steadied himself, broke forward and launched a right footed missile shot past Hopkinson to put North End one up from around 12 yards out.

The crowd went into delirium. What a fantastic physical effort from the centre forward with a rugby prop's physique.

"Daw-son Daw-son," they bellowed - and rightly so - by the end of the season their hero had returned North End - *in league matches alone* - 61 goals from 101 career appearances. Without a shadow of a doubt he would have been worth millions today...

All the crowd noise had no effect on the Bolton team whatsoever. They professionally stuck to their task and within a few minutes Wyn Davies had spurned a chance to bring 'The Trotters' back to parity. This was followed by Lee setting up the hardworking Hill, but his shot was parried to safety by Kelly.

Indeed it was now Bolton controlling proceedings, and in the last ten minutes of the half Kelly was called upon to make superb saves from Dave Lennard and Peter Deakin when it seemed certain Bolton would equalise.

The half time whistle blew just after Davies had headed past Kelly but over the bar from a cross by Gordon Taylor. What a 45 minutes that had been; the players rightfully applauded off the pitch as they retired to the dressing rooms.

Dawson bursts through to score North End's first against Bolton in the FA Cup replay at Deepdale

The second half began just as the first had – with Preston going gung ho at the Bolton defence.

Shots rained in on the Bolton goal from Dawson, Lawton Spavin and Wilson, but were either off target or not good enough to pass

Hopkinson. After around 10 minutes, Bolton won a corner on the left. From Taylor's cross, centre half Edwards - unmarked at the near post - nodded the ball home to almost a deafening silence.

North End captain Nobby Lawton crashes home the winner against Bolton in the FA Cup replay at Deepdale

Kelly looked around at his defenders, now with their heads bowed, seeming to ask where was the cover?

The goal signaled a period of Bolton domination, their confidence completely renewed.

Lee almost wriggled through, before a last gasp Singleton tackle on Davies as he was about to shoot saved North End's bacon. The pattern continued up until the last quarter of an hour of the game, when North End finally regained the lead with a somewhat scrambled goal.

Holden, leaving Dave Hatton behind as he cut infield threaded the ball to Godfrey who passed it on to Wilson on the right. The winger fired in a teasing first time cross which Lawton and Hopkinson were trying to get to, but for hugely different reasons. Screams of anticipation from the crowd turned into a massive roar of delight as Lawton finally managed to bring the ball under control long enough to ram the ball home from close range.

With time ticking away and the crowd calling for full time, Bolton had the ball cleared off the North End line with Kelly beaten. So, when the referee finally blew the whistle the loud cheer of the crowd was a mixture of joy, excitement and relief.

Once again North End had 'delivered' with some style in this quite remarkable season.

Surely there would be less tension against Carlisle United?

17   TOO CLOSE FOR COMFORT

PRESTON NORTH END 1 CARLISLE UNITED 0
FA CUP 5TH ROUND 15/2/1964

'The 90 mile Derby,' probably the most unique game of its type in English football, saw Preston North End and Carlisle United gather up their 'local' fans from as far south as Standish to Dumfiries on the Scottish borders.

All tickets were sold for the game at Deepdale which pitted North End against the Division Four high flyers from Cumbria, playing in the fifth round for the very first time.

They possessed a free scoring centre forward in Hugh McIlmoyle who was in fact the leading goal scorer in the country at the time. He would become something of a footballing nomad, scoring freely wherever he plied his trade - indeed, after another seven years had ticked by he would actually join North End's ranks in the Alan Ball Senior era.

With Smith still not available, once more North End went with:-

Kelly, Ross, Davidson, Lawton, Singleton, Kendall, Wilson, Godfrey, Dawson, Spavin, Holden.

With a sea of humanity crammed into Deepdale - the official crowd recorded at 37,161 - Carlisle kicked off towards the Spion Kop. Up for the task, the visitors were full of life and when Singleton fluffed a clearance in the first minute it let in the dangerous McIlmoyle, whose snap shot was deflected for a corner by Kelly. Kelly was badly upended in the act of collecting the corner and needed to spend a few minutes being treated by the healing hands of Walter Crook before he felt able to carry on.

In the meantime, 'McIlmoyle/9/Carlisle' became the first entry in the referees book for the challenge on the keeper.

The visitors were keen to impress and were aggressive in their play. North End seemed somewhat taken aback and rattled by these upstarts from Division Four.

Preston could hardly progress past half way before they were back on their heels. Sammy Taylor, the ex North End winger of a few seasons before, was having an excellent game back at his old stamping ground. He was murdering left back Davidson, creating a chance for inside forward Joe Livingstone before trying his luck himself from 20 yards.

On the quarter hour mark, North End had an escape when Taylor delivered a corner directly and with the minimum of fuss to Livingstone whose lightening header went narrowly wide of the top corner.

North End seemed to be fire fighting all over the pitch as the visitors made a mockery of their league standing.

Out of the blue, Dawson fired in a 25 yard missile strike that caught Ian Ross in the Carlisle goal completely unawares. In a desperate movement he managed to palm the ball against the post and away to safety.

Taylor brought the ball forward - again, gave Davidson the slip - again, and crossed beautifully for McIlmoyle whose attempted header on goal was denied by a Kendall interception at the last moment.

Slowly but surely, North End began to creep into the game, as quite understandably, the visitors opening salvo began to take its toll.

Wilson finally created some room by skinning Terry Caldwell, the United left back. His inside pass to Spavin was wasted by the midfielder however, the attempted strike on goal being collected by the crowd ten yards wide to the right of goal.

The change in the direction of the game was palpable for all to see, and Lawton suddenly became midfield's prominent operator. He was continually feeding Wilson the ball, but the winger was seeing no reward for his efforts in teeing up the forwards.

With the Carlisle aggression now contained, North End had a more composed look about them. The outcome was that they dealt the first blow of the game after 26 minutes.

The visitors simply paid the price for allowing Wilson too much room. The winger passed inside to Dawson, who sliced his shot badly, the ball spinning towards the byline but not crossing it, half way between the goal post and corner flag. Ever alert, Wilson retrieved the ball and crossed for Dawson once more whose attempt was blocked. The ball was only half cleared and fell to Spavin who drove the ball home with power inside the near post.

With the lead obtained and North End settled, Kendall caught the eye demonstrating a reading and understanding of the game well in advance of his years.

Wilson was continuing to plague Caldwell, on one occasion leaving him rooted as he cut in, only to blast his shot wide. He then played Godfrey in, whose fierce curling drive necessitated a desperate acrobatic save from goalkeeper Ian Ross to deny the goal.

At the back, Singleton now had McIlmoyle under his control and right back George Ross was completely dominating the anonymous Frank Kirkup - the winger losing every battle to the speedy full back.

Half time arrived and North End were thankful of their lead against game opponents.

After an early Carlisle move was broken up by Singleton, North End sped up field. A long cross field pass by Godfrey to Wilson was neatly centred in an instant to the waiting Dawson, whose header was only denied goal status by the scrambling keeper,Ross. To their credit, Carlisle didn't lie down. With Taylor, Livingstone and McIlmoyle all very lively, the North End defence had to have their wits about them.

SPAVIN STRIKES !

Alan Spavin drives the ball home past the outstretched leg of the Carlisle Utd defender in the FA Cup 5th Round tie at Deepdale

Play fluctuated, but it was the Carlisle supporters who gasped with relief as Wilson, with his well worked shimmy, cut inside after a Godfrey pass and drove a lovely rising shot narrowly over the angle of post and bar.

McIlmoyle then broke promisingly forward for Carlisle only to be unceremoniously brought to earth by Singleton - the centre half having his name immediately entered below McIlmoyle's in the referee's notebook. The visitors were coming to prominence again, increasingly buzzing around North End's box. This was a good spell for Carlisle, they were giving North End's attack no room to play and keeping the pressure on with a high back line.

In fact they almost equalised when Livingstone set McIlmoyle clear. Leaving Singleton in his wake, his centre was met by Taylor running in - the venomous shot first hitting Kelly's right post, then ricocheting directly across to the left post before being hurriedly cleared.

Now it was the North End fans who were gasping with relief... and while they were, Carlisle's Reg Davies, running alongside Nobby Lawton turned to him and said, *"With that luck, you'll probably win the cup now!"*

As the half progressed, both teams saw their attacking moves peter out as defences remained on top. Credit must go to the visitors who had stifled the North End all round goal scoring threat, but had come up just short as the final whistle blew.

After the excitement of the Nottingham Forest and Bolton Wanderers ties, North End were never really at their best in this game, but a place in the quarter finals had been booked nevertheless, in a sea of nervous tension.

'Cup Fever' was endemic in Preston...

18   OXFORD BLUES

OXFORD UNITED 1 PRESTON NORTH END 2
FA CUP 6TH ROUND 29/2/1964

The sleepy city of Oxford was loudly awoken and completely swamped by FA Cup football fanatics on Leap Year Day, 1964.

Oxford United, the newest club in the Football League at the time, were having a great time. The Division Four club had reached the dizzy heights of the FA Cup quarter finals, and had drawn Preston North End at home - a club steeped in FA Cup tradition.

Proving once again that the FA Cup favours no team, Oxford had liquidated Division One high flyers Blackburn Rovers by 3-1 at home in the previous round - so had to be respected and taken seriously by North End.

With the gates locked a full hour before the kick off with 22,750 shoehorned inside the Manor Ground, excitement was at fever pitch as the teams ran out. *Both* teams had glory within their grasp.

With Kendall and Smith unavailable, North End fielded:-

Kelly, Ross, Donnelly, Lawton, Singleton, Davidson, Wilson, Godfrey, Dawson, Spavin, Holden.

The weather was dull, still and mild with the pitch having little grass on it. Lawton and Ron Atkinson tossed up and a huge roar from the expectant crowd anticipated the referees whistle to signal the start of proceedings.

Oxford won the first corner, to sustained cheering and applause. The ball, cleared initially by Davidson was returned immediately by John Shuker, his hopeful punt into the penalty area giving Kelly his first feel of the ball.

There were signs in Oxford's play that they were adopting similar tactics to those of Carlisle United – who North End had great difficulty seeing off in the last round. Their aggression didn't flummox North End though and after an assertive flurry of attacking play, they took the lead in the seventh minute.

Given plenty of room to operate in Spavin floated a lovely ball over the square United back line which found Dawson, having sprung the offside trap, in space.

Chesting the ball down and forwards, he homed in on goal and bustled the ball in from close range. Becoming the meat in a defender and goalkeeper sandwich proved no obstacle to the North End powerhouse.

Dawson in the process of putting North End ahead against Oxford United

This was Dawson's fourth goal of the 1964 FA Cup campaign, and startlingly, his 32nd of the season - a stunning performance.

Oxford hustled but North End gave the impression they were always in charge. Singleton was a tower of strength in defence, controlling the back line with authority. In fact, so confident were North End becoming, they were keeping the ball for long periods with neat inter passing - Spavin and Holden being particularly adept at this. This was in stark contrast to the hosts style of play, which was an enthusiastic *'get into them'* at every opportunity.

Wilson set up Godfrey nicely, but he shot tamely wide. Lawton centred for Dawson who controlled the ball superbly, only to watch his inventive lob go just over the bar.

Oxford had by now assigned two defenders to Dawson, and it was they who combined to see off an excellent Ross centre aimed at the big Scot.

After 35 minutes, the first real shot of note at the Preston goal was drilled in by Atkinson, but Kelly patted it down with no difficulty. The home side desperately needed a lift as every move forward they made hit the rocks - otherwise known as the North End defence. There had been some time and thought applied to Preston's tactical set up and its flawless performance was driving Oxford to despair. United Centre forward Bill Calder had not won a single header when contesting with Singleton, who was the surest footed player on the pitch.

The home crowd tried their best to rally the team by bellowing the repetitive chant of Ox-ford, Ox-ford, Ox-ford every time they were in possession. It was the 3,000 North End fans who cheered the loudest just before half time, however.

Holden, moving swiftly down the left threaded a pass into the area for Godfrey to run onto. With Oxford preoccupied with marking Dawson, the inside right had enough space and time to draw Harry Fearnley from his goal before sweeping a powerful left foot shot into the net. It was a cold, ruthless but skilled piece of football and sent North End into the sheds with a two goal lead they thoroughly deserved.

During the break North End manager, Jimmy Milne, was surely warning his players what to expect. United had to recover a two goal deficit within the next 45 minutes. With simply nothing to lose, this all pointed to an almighty Oxford siege being laid on the North End goal from the resumption.

The home side didn't disappoint.

Out they flew, tenacious and menacing. Harrying any North Ender within a sniff of the ball, their renewed vigour was drawing loud cheers of appreciation from the home crowd. North End withstood this initial assault of fury, with no chinks visible just yet in their defensive armour.

Godfrey ends a fine move by scoring North End's second at the Manor Ground

A bad pass made under pressure by Davidson, was fortunately retrieved by Holden and the danger was averted. Ross then had to make a last gasp tackle on Shuker as he attempted to burst through the North End line.

While Oxford kept on slamming the ball fruitlessly down the middle for Calder - he was still being well marshaled by Singleton - North End were opting to play through the Spavin/Holden conduit on the left. It gave Spavin the latitude to link play from the backs to the attack, and he was reveling in the role.

Then, on the hour Oxford finally halved the deficit. For the second time in a minute a marauding pack of gold shirted players swept towards the North End penalty area. As the throng entered the box the ball was flicked on by Atkinson to Tony Jones, barging his way past defenders to the ball and poking it past Kelly into the net.

The expected onslaught had borne fruit, now North End would have to stand firm under twice the pressure as Oxford tails were well and truly up. Oxford attacked fanatically. Ross twice denied Colin Harrington further progress as he approached the danger area and Arthur Longbottom's vicious drive was but a yard wide. Jones then lunged at a ball played across the six yard box but failed to connect by inches.

They were certainly floundering when a desperate outstretched Lawton foot just about diverted an Atkinson shot wide and a Jones back header went just past the post. With this series of near misses, the crowd noise was deafening and increased the nerve wracking feeling off the scale for the North End fans.

Kelly watches the ball flash past his post during a spell of Oxford pressure

This sustained assault continued, and another Oxford posse arrived in the North End box kicking out at everything that moved, the ball eventually grasped and hugged tight by Kelly after bouncing off countless legs.

The North End fans could hardy look. Some form of containment was needed - and quick! Unfortunately, more of the same was heaped on and how such a period of domination could go unrewarded was beyond belief.

Finally with around ten minutes left, North End poked their noses out past the half way line and started to play some football. Dawson played in Godfrey for a shot but he couldn't take it in his stride, Holden then put Dawson through but a linesman was already flagging for offside.

With the ball now predominantly at the Oxford end, the gusto started to diminish from the home team.

North End had just about prevailed in this 'game of two halves' which turned out to be the most severe examination yet of their FA Cup run.

Oxford deserved a replay, but it was North End's name that was in the velvet bag for the Monday lunchtime draw…

Draw for the semis

- North End v Swansea at Villa Park, Birmingham
- West Ham v Manchester Utd. or Sunderland at Hillsborough, Sheffield

Division II club must play at Wembley

Norwich, Deepdale evening kick-off

By WALTER PILKINGTON

PRESTON NORTH END have played Swansea only once in the Cup and that was recent enough for every supporter to remember it.

…and was the first drawn out; the Lilywhites being given the best possible chance to reach Wembley by being paired with Swansea Town thereby avoiding West Ham United and either Manchester United or Sunderland.

19   MUD, GLORIOUS MUD

PRESTON NORTH END 2 SWANSEA TOWN 1
FA CUP SEMI FINAL 14/3/1964

Total dedication and a basin full of endurance was needed to obtain a ticket to watch North End in the Villa Park semi-final.

All-night queues of the North End faithful formed around Deepdale in the quest to buy that little piece of card from the club in exchange for a minimum of 5/- (25p), which meant they would be entitled to stand on the Villa Park terraces and (hopefully) cheer on their heroes to Wembley. North End shifted in excess of 20,000 tickets of mixed denominations.

The day dawned, and it rained and rained and rained. Solidly, persistently. It was no different following the pilgrimage to Villa Park - soaked to the skin fans clicking through the turnstiles to see the roofless terraces overlooking a flat bed of mud with standing pools of water dotted hither and thither - in the unrelenting heavy rainfall.

News came through of countless postponements up and down the country due to the all encompassing torrential rain, but the word at Villa Park was that the all second division FA Cup Semi Final would go ahead.

'Sensational Swansea' having defeated Liverpool at Anfield in the quarter final and taken three out of four league points from North End in 63/64, brought with them an estimated 10,000 more followers than North End, amazing for a club struggling to average 9,000 for a home league game. Apparently this was due to a strong Welsh presence in the

'Black Country' and other closet fans who just wanted to be present for this decider.

North End fielded the same team that edged home at Oxford, with the exception of Ashworth replacing Godfrey:-

Kelly, Ross, Donnelly, Lawton, Singleton, Davidson, Wilson, Ashworth, Dawson, Spavin, Holden.

A couple of the North End players chatting to the fans after getting a pre-match feel of the stadium reported that the pitch was soft on top but firm underneath; the ideal recipe for a skid pan.

'Change kits' were to be used by both sides so North End would grace Villa Park in their royal blue shirts, while Swansea would be sporting an orange top. Both teams would have white shorts.

The teams eventually ran down the tunnel and into the pelting rain to be welcomed by a massive roar from both sets of supporters. The excitement and expectation of all inside the stadium was almost tangible. Just 90 minutes away from the FA Cup Final...

Losing a semi final – any semi final – is the worst feeling ever. Far worse than being competition runners up, for at least a part in the final has been played. Tommy Docherty was right - on this occasion at least - when he said, *"You get nowt for being second,"* but even that grim reality statement paradoxically recognises that you were at least the runners-up. The semi final is the one last game when two teams are scrambling to reach the centre piece event; the stakes massively high.

The North End team realised the situation. They would never have a better chance of experiencing the glory of Wembley than this; it was every player's dream back then. As Tony Singleton prophetically said to the press when asked for a quote as the team left Preston, *"We must and have to win. No excuses."*

The dull, wet and murky conditions didn't add anything to the spectacle for the spectator and within a couple of minutes of the start the playing 'surface' was as cut up as any waterlogged cow meadow. Passes were immediately going astray from North End, failing to navigate those puddles that were littered all over the pitch. As North End's was a passing game, this didn't bode at all well.

The first real excitement was a speed test between Ross and Jimmy Mclaughlin down the wing, Ross winning comfortably and giving Kelly an early feel of the ball.

Swansea appeared to be more the more adaptable in the early exchanges, hoofing the ball through the rain rather than the mud and usually reaching the intended targets.

On one such occasion a cross was curled in from the right and met well by centre forward Eddie Thomas, but the header went wide of Kelly's post.

A through ball then split the North End defence putting Keith Todd away, dashing towards last man Kelly with Lawton in hot pursuit. A supreme effort by the North End captain resulted in a tackle executed a yard shy of the penalty area - deemed a foul by the referee - Todd sliding forward on his backside a further ten yards towards the advancing Kelly. Herbie Williams struck the free kick hard and low but just wide of Kelly's left post.

Having 'weathered' the early Swansea onslaught, North End finally moved forward. Lawton skillfully lobbed the ball into the goalmouth, Dawson charged onto it, but his header was collected safely by Noel Dwyer in the Swansea goal.

Spavin then had a chance on goal, but his attempt to volley home a dropping ball was completely mistimed and ended with a weak shot just about rolling through to Dwyer.

North End looked like they were finally settling down, appearing increasingly commanding under pressure, as demonstrated when the buzzing Lawton was caught out of position but covered promptly and efficiently by Ross, calmly relieving the mud covered Todd of the ball with ease and assurance. Ross was proving to be North End's most prominent defender; his competence - and confidence - in the abysmal conditions being a real comfort to North End. A lovely move, albeit designed for firmer ground, was orchestrated by Lawton and Dawson but the final pass never reached Ashworth - the ball coming to grief in a muddy puddle some five yards shy of the on rushing forward.

North End's spell of ascendency was broken when Donnelly failed to collect a cross field pass letting winger Barrie Jones advance down the wing behind him. His centre was met by Thomas, whose powerful downwards header went inches wide with Kelly beaten.

With Swansea spirits duly lifted, the next few minutes brought a series of crosses for Kelly to deal with - which he did with the minimum of fuss.

Ross and McLaughlin were still going head to head on Swansea's left flank. As both chased a through pass the inevitable occurred on the slippery surface and both went sprawling, arms and legs everywhere; McLaughlin emerging with a noticeable limp which brought a smile to faces of the North End fans in the crowd.

Rain was still falling and North End's passing game was still suffering as potential openings were being squandered in the boggy conditions. While this remained the status quo, Swansea could never be ruled out of this game.

Lawton was at his feisty best. Involved in everything, and vocally directing advancements and retreats, this was an unassuming but star performer.

Another spell of Swansea pressure developed, three attacks on the bounce being diffused by Ross, Singleton and Davidson in that order.

North End moved forward, and Ashworth launched a terrific shot at goal that could well have brought reward had it not caught a defenders shoulder along the way. The subsequent melee in front of the Swansea goal following the corner was eventually hacked clear.

A strange incident occurred shortly afterwards that probably cost North End the lead. Ashworth was called offside after a good move had left the big striker homing in on goal. Following vociferous North End protesting, the referee finally consulted his linesman who it seemed agreed with North End – he had completely overlooked the fact that full back Brian Hughes was anchored behind his goalkeeper on the Swansea goal line, playing Ashworth onside!

Suitably chastised, the referee ordered a 'bounce' which, under the terms of the *Law of Sod*, was duly cleared instantly by Swansea.

Donnelly and Ross look on as Kelly palms a point blank header to safety in the Villa Park gloom

Swansea didn't appear as scientific in their play as North End, but were full of grit and determination. They were adept too at packing their defence very quickly when necessary, thus smothering many North End possibilities.

After one such occurrence just before half time, the ball was played down North End's left by Swansea right back Roy Evans. Evans had proved himself to be something of a useful player, setting the Welshmen quickly on the attack on numerous occasions. His pass found inside forward Derek Draper, who put in a high teasing cross that drew Kelly from his goal. Under challenge, he could only punch clear as far as Thomas stood near the penalty spot. He nodded the ball left to McLaughlin, who turned and shot first time across the face of goal burying the ball in the far corner.

The noise was deafening. A plethora of homemade cardboard leeks, daffodils and swans were immediately thrust in the air and waved about in sheer delight.

There was just time for Ashworth to head over at the other end before the referee blew the half time whistle. Neither team deserved to be losing, but did Swansea deserve to be winning? It was a little tough on North End, but the boundless enthusiasm of Swansea had been rewarded at the perfect moment meaning North End manager Jimmy Milne would have to deliver a different speech than he had planned at half time.

A little more urgency was evident in North End's play after the break. Two speedy Wilson sorties down the right had resulted in crosses aimed at Dawson, but the battering ram could not made them count.

However, Dawson and indeed North End, got lucky in the 52nd minute. Fifteen yards out and moving across the penalty area he was manhandled by 'Swans' centre half Brian Purcell and the referee some 15 yards up field, blew for a spot kick without hesitation.

Dawson usually blasted his penalties in like something launched from Mission Control in Houston, but on this occasion was a little more circumspect. Dawson later recalled, *"I had smashed my last penalty over the bar, and realized I had to be more careful. Trainer Walter Crook couldn't watch me take this one."* He knew he had to deliver, so placed his drive hard, low and true to Dwyer's right. It hit the back of the net with Dwyer still in mid air.

Much North End relief all round, and now back on level terms. Energised, North End dominated for a period. However, Swansea were still packing their defence at very short notice and generally being successful in denying North End access to Dwyer's goal; the 'Lilywhites' still well overcooking their play when simplicity was called for.

There is only so much chasing and harrying that you can do on a swamp however, and it was noticeable that a few Swansea players had their hands on their hips at any break in the play. With North End seeing more of the ball, Swansea were beginning to bend under the pressure. The Welshmen owed a lot to the tireless work of Purcell and Hughes at the back that was keeping North End at arm's length.

Dawson equalises from the penalty spot against Swansea at Villa Park

Some North End dilly dallying invited Swansea back into attack; Davidson the guilty party, trying to pass his way through the mud when a good old fashioned clearance was all that was needed. It was up to Lawton to bail him and the team out at the cost of a foul.

After 71 minutes, Singleton scored one of the most remarkable and unlikely semi final goals in history to put North End ahead.

With the ball finally and somewhat desperately cleared from the Swansea box to around 30 yards from their goal line. Davidson won a challenge and scrambled the ball forward to Spavin. Pursued by Williams, the link man pushed the ball back towards the high North End line of players. Effectively, he teed up Singleton beautifully to swing his left boot through the ball and see the resulting missile hit the back of the net a second or so later. The Swansea 'keeper Dwyer was rendered agog. That breathtaking long range strike by Preston born Singleton was his first for his hometown club – and what a goal it was!

Swansea, now with nothing at all to lose, attacked Preston wherever and whenever possible, with sheer desperation in their play.

This was largely dealt with by North End but as time ran out centre half

Tony Singleton's speculative shot sails past Dwyer, the Swansea goalkeeper

Singleton conceded a free kick. The resulting cross caused utter panic in the North End defence with the ball bouncing wildly about before being hoofed clear. It was duly returned straight away and headed goalward by Thomas.

Kelly collected the ball calmly and made his way forward off the goal line only to be deliberately barged to the ground by the aforementioned Thomas, no doubt frustrated at another opportunity being denied. Davidson was first on the scene ready to take matters into his own hands until Donnelly sensibly blocked him and Lawton off from getting involved any further.

The whistle blew and North End were in the FA Cup Final. What a fantastic achievement for the Division Two team and Jimmy Milne, the manager - who had already experienced two North End Wembley FA Cup Finals, in 1938 as a player and 1954 as the trainer.

Alan Kelly is surrounded by his defenders after being barged to the ground by Eddie Thomas

Dawson at his wonderful, unrelenting best – powering a header towards goal past the flailing arms of Dwyer, the Swansea goalkeeper

The Villa Park semi final through the eyes and pen of the very gifted illustrator, Bob Bond. There is no bigger North End fan than Bob, and he often created such features for football magazines and comics of the time.

20   MARCH, APRIL & MAY

FA CUP FINAL BUILD UP 1964

It's worth reflecting at this point just what the North End fans had enjoyed up to the middle of March during the 1963/64 season.

As well as booking an appearance at Wembley in the FA Cup Final with all that that entails, the team hadn't exactly neglected their weekly league duties either!

Proudly standing third in Division Two, the whole stunning season had seemingly come from nowhere, following on as it did from two seasons of distinctly bland play and average results.

Something had certainly clicked into place. It was a combination of a few things - the maturing of the youth system players of early 60's vintage; Dawson finally flourishing fully into his role with comforting support from Godfrey and Ashworth but surely, above all, it was the arrival of Lawton towards the end of the previous season that was the glue holding all these positive factors together.

Lawton was a very good player. Born in Manchester and making the grade for his local team Manchester United, he was beginning to make his mark when he broke his leg. Despite making a full recovery, he eventually was squeezed out of the first team by the presence of Pat Crerand, signed from Celtic.

Very modest in nature, Norbert 'Nobby' Lawton had something of an inferiority complex when a youngster at Old Trafford.

"When I was a kid at United I used to watch the Busby Babes train, legends like Duncan Edwards and Tommy Taylor, and I thought if these blokes are the professionals then I've no chance. I was never fiercely ambitious, and deep down I didn't think I'd make it."

His transfer to North End was managed with care by Busby, who knew all about Preston, their manager, their football brand and philosophy. He had sold Dawson to Preston in October 1961, rather than to Division One rivals Liverpool who had also expressed an interest. By coincidence, Dawson and Lawton were great friends and the latter's arrival at Deepdale must have lifted Dawson's spirits.

Nobby Lawton

The fee for Lawton's services of £11,500 (today's value £217,000), was money very well spent. Arguably North End's finest post-war captain, Lawton certainly lost all those nagging footballing inhibitions while he was at Deepdale. Under Jimmy Milne, he soon became a stylish, goalscoring and vocal fetch-and-carry link between defence and attack, relishing the responsibility of his new captaincy role.

Lawton could certainly tackle hard and mix it when necessary too - all the time with his distinctive running style of left arm bent at the elbow as though mimicking a matador. His role could probably be best described as the blueprint for Bryan Robson's function when he led Manchester United, some 20 years later.

Lawton described his friend Dawson as, *"a bull of a centre-forward, a Deepdale hero."* He wasn't wrong; by the time the semi final against

Swansea Town had been won he had bagged 33 goals in this epic season.

He was a centre forward that dreams are made of. He would just about do anything to put the ball in the net for North End; his commitment to the cause never in question.

With the classic 'PP' shirt crest seemingly bulging out of his chest, he struck fear and dread into nervous opposition defences, their preoccupation on how to cope with him often letting in his strike partner, be it Godfrey or Ashworth, to profit.

The early 60's youth system had produced four players of note that by 1963 were stepping up to the mark - George Ross, Alan Spavin, Howard Kendall and David Wilson.

Alex Dawson

Kendall was sheer class. He played football like a veteran when he was just 17 years old, and surely he must have been worth at least one England cap during his playing career. He left North End for Everton at the ripe old age of 20, having already racked up over 100 appearances, not to mention 13 goals from midfield.

Ross would go on to become a foundation stone for future years. Quick, efficient and supremely loyal to North End through little thick and lots of thin, he was Mr. Dependable. A succession of managers made him their first choice, which speaks volumes.

Spavin was like fine wine - he got better with age. He read a game so very well, and his passing was imperious. How many uncapped Division Three players approaching the age of 30 would be singled out by the national coach and told that their performance was 'outstanding'?

The name 'Wilson' figures all over this book. The match reports concerning his performances in certain games are simply sensational.

Already knowledgeable folk are talking of Preston's DAVID WILSON as "another Tom Finney" and certainly he has a big reputation to uphold. The signs are that he will be in the England international side before long.

Soccer Star Magazine, February 22nd, 1964

Magazines, newspapers and North End away programmes of the time repeatedly hailed him as a player of the future and he became Alf Ramsey's choice as deputy to Terry Paine; the England coach eventually capping Wilson seven times at U23 level.

By March 1964, Wilson had played in three of those U23 Internationals, and was a joy to watch on the North End right wing.

Following the fantastic semi final win over Swansea Town, North End thumped Norwich City 3-0 at Deepdale on the following Tuesday evening to leave the Division Two table looking like this :-

		P	W	D	L	F	A	PTS
1	Leeds United	34	18	13	3	56	29	49
2	Sunderland	34	20	8	6	63	30	48
3	**Preston North End**	34	19	9	6	68	43	47

Sadly, the glorious season of 1963/64, or more poignantly still - the entire 60's - would never get better than at this moment...

The next game, just a week after experiencing the dizzy heights of reaching the FA Cup Final, was to be a plunging low.

It was an away game at Roker Park against arch rivals for promotion, Sunderland. North End simply had to bring something home from this game.

They did ... shell shock!

North End were 4-0 down at half time, ambushed, pummeled and put to the sword by a rampant home team desperate to put daylight between the two clubs. It was a minor miracle that North End prevented further damage in the second half, but they did and travelled back to Deepdale with plenty to think about.

A great Easter saw three wins on the bounce, as the team obviously tried to gather themselves, and it enabled the team and importantly their fans to keep fading promotion hopes alive.

However, a 4-2 defeat at Millmoor by Rotherham United on April 4th finally put the tin hat on any thoughts of promotion.

The last four games of the season brought just three points from a possible eight, North End finishing a memorable league campaign five points behind runners-up Sunderland and in all truth with something of a whimper. The final Division Two table shows that of the top three, only North End lost games during the final month of the season.

<u>25th April 1964</u>

		P	W	D	L	F	A	PTS
1	Leeds United	42	24	15	3	71	34	63
2	Sunderland	42	25	11	6	81	37	61
3	**Preston North End**	42	23	10	9	79	54	56

North End's form, therefore, was not ideal as the last big battle of the season loomed up – the FA Cup Final.

Howard Kendall, George Ross, David Wilson and Alex Dawson along with the Morecambe Dairy Maid in a pre FA Cup Final publicity photograph

As April drew to a close, the media started to 'hype up' the FA Cup Final. It was soon patently obvious where the gentlemen of the national press thought the trophy would end up - in London of course - at Upton Park, where else?

It was hard to argue with their 'logical' train of thought. West Ham United - 'The Entertainers' - comfortably placed in Division One, would surely account for Division Two promotion bridesmaids Preston North End.

Then, even more depressing news filtered out of the Preston camp. Ian Davidson, North End's left half and certain to appear at Wembley, was suddenly and mysteriously suspended by the club.

No details have ever been released as to exactly why, but whatever the episode was it marked the beginning of the end for the Scot, as relations between the player and the club were never the same again.

Davidson was eventually transferred to Middlesbrough, and while he was there gave an interview to *'Football Monthly'* about the pre-cup final 'incident.'

In a feature entitled, ***'IDIOT! ….that's what I thought when I missed the cup final'*** Davidson recalled the shock waves that travelled the length and breadth of the football world when his suspension was announced.

"My misdemeanour also brought fame to the then 17 year Howard Kendall who took my place in the final, perhaps the only good thing to come out of the event - which led to my refusal to re-sign for Preston during the summer. I eventually came to terms with myself, and the club for the 64/65 season, and for 16 games was back in my old position having been refused a transfer request. Then without warning, I found that I was on the list - resulting in my move to the north east. It was a sad end to my time in Lancashire."

North End's progress in the time he was at Deepdale is noted and obviously pleased Davidson, but the rest of the article is tinged with feelings of sadness.

"It was a great pity, for until my unfortunate lapse a few days before the final it had been a great season for the club and me. That magnificent cup run was certainly the highlight of my career and I have only myself to blame for the stupid circumstances that prevented me from treading the famous Wembley turf. What I did was quite idiotic and completely indefensible. I deserved to be punished and prepared to take it on the

chin. I was full of regrets, but the suspension of 14 days was a thing I could, and did accept. But I was very hurt by the fact that, even though many people thought my sentence justifiable, I was dropped from the cup final team. I felt a complete idiot."

BUNKERED!

CAREFREE finalists football - cum - golf as these Preston North End players lightheartedly kick the ball from a bunker during a training session on the golf course at Oatlands Park Hotel, Weybridge, Surrey today. Left to right, goalkeeper Alan Kelly, centre half Tony Singleton, and inside left Alan Spavin.

The Davidson saga overshadowed another major change in the North End line up; left back John Donnelly was to make way for the return of Jim Smith, who hadn't featured in the cup run since the third round tie against Nottingham Forest at the City Ground.

The North End squad travelled down to the Oatlands Park Hotel, Weybridge a few days before the big game to prepare for the task ahead and enjoy a break from all the pre-match hype. It was to be hoped that the players had avoided viewing the national press.....

On the other hand, back in that last week of April 64, young Howard Kendall couldn't quite believe what was happening...he was about to become the youngest player ever to participate in a FA Cup Final at just 17 years and 245 days. *"My father was only saying the other night that I should forget all about the final and then I wouldn't be too disappointed. Now this has happened, I am too delighted for words. I just walked in from a training session and there was the cup final team pinned up on the notice board in the Deepdale reception. It just read: H Kendall – number 6. It was a complete surprise, I was stunned. I don't think it will bother me that much...I certainly hope not!"*

West Ham United — Claret and Blue shirts, White shorts
STANDEN Goal · BOND R-Back · BURKETT L-Back · BOVINGTON R-Half · BROWN C-Half · MOORE L-Half · BRABROOK O-Right · BOYCE I-Right · BYRNE C-Forward · HURST I-Left · SISSONS O-Left

Preston North End — White shirts, Dark Blue shorts
KELLY Goal · ROSS R-Back · SMITH L-Back · LAWTON R-Half · SINGLETON C-Half · KENDALL L-Half · WILSON O-Right · ASHWORTH I-Right · DAWSON C-Forward · SPAVIN I-Left · HOLDEN O-Left

Wembley just made for their method

Sketches by BALLON

WEST HAM TO DO IT—IN STYLE!

BY putting on the style and winning well at Wembley today, West Ham can hand out a lesson to ...

West Ham to win
says RALPH JACKSON

WEST HAM UNITED have only to repeat their semi-final performance against Manchester United to ensure victory in convincing fashion. On that rain-soaked day at Hillsborough, the ...mers displayed an outstanding brand of soccer in ...

I AM SORRY, PRESTON, BUT IT WILL BE WEST HAM!

THE last time Preston went to Wembley they were favourites. Almost witted football that is at last being laced ...

The lack of respect for North End was becoming ridiculous. However, after a while these type of headlines can have a strangely galvanizing effect on those on the receiving end of such flawed assessments, and every North End fan was hoping this was the case.

News from North End's Surrey camp was upbeat, with the players reported to be 'settled' and looking forward to the prospect of taking part in the final.

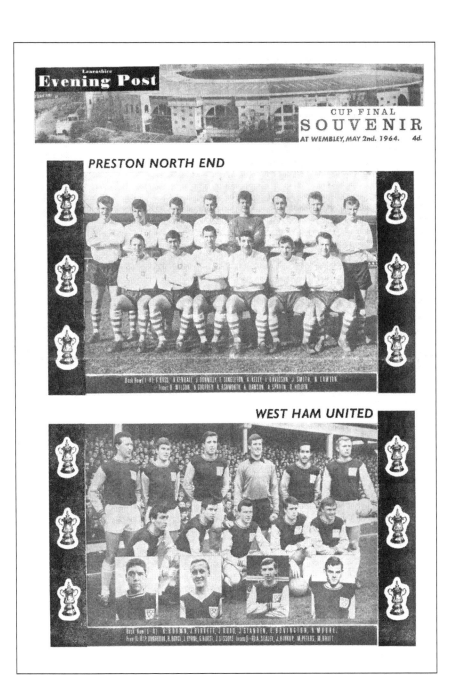

The Lancashire Evening Post (LEP) FA Cup Final Preview newspaper 'Souvenir Edition'

A different type of *'Evening Post'* FA Cup Final souvenir went on sale; a magazine that had each of the North End squad offering their opinion on a fellow team mate.

Dawson's take on Lawton is glowing. *'The Black Prince'* could certainly see the value of his long time friend and colleague.

TRIBUTE TO A GREAT SKIPPER

— Nobby Lawton

By *ALEX DAWSON*

So it has fallen to me . . . the severe task of talking about our skipper at North-End my old mate Nobby Lawton.

What an opportunity to put myself in the captain's good books! What an opportunity to say "Nobby . . . you are the greatest!"

Seriously though, if I had been asked to write about one player in Britain, my choice would have been the same. And I doubt if there's a more qualified player than Alex Dawson to talk about him.

Nobby and myself played together in Manchester United's Youth team and graduated to the reserves. Since he arrived at Deepdale we have always "roomed" together on away trips.

And few people realise that I had a lot to do with him coming to Preston. Our manager Jimmy Milne and I saw United Reserves beat Preston Reserves 7—1 one night and he turned to me and asked: "Who would you sign out of that lot?"

I replied without hesitation: "Nobby Lawton." Because I know that this guy can play and would never let anybody down, in football or anywhere.

Nobby Lawton is among the top three right-halves in England in my book. He has that rare combination of class PLUS bite.

When Mr. Milne appointed him captain it was the best thing that ever happened to Preston and Nobby. He is one of these people who thrive on responsibility. He's a stern task-master on that field but completely fair. The great team-spirit at Preston would not have been the same without him.

Nobby Lawton.

MAY 2 Saturday ABC

---Big Afternoon Out---

Independent Television Presents the two greatest sporting attractions of the day

1.14 Professional Wrestling

FROM Wembley Town Hall
As arrangements made before Panoramarama Ltd
The top men of the ring in one big bill. Including the long awaited tag team match between these two teams who both claim to be the great unbeatables

STEVE LOGAN (Brixton) and
MICK McMANUS (New Cross)
VERSUS

VIC FAULKNER (Bolton) and
BERT ROYAL (Bolton)
and you also see some of the following masters of the mat
HEAVYWEIGHT
GOMEZ MAX MILLIANO (Peru)
VERSUS
JOHNNY CZESLAW (Poland)
WELTERWEIGHT
JOE MURPHY (Dublin)
VERSUS
AL NICOL (Nottingham)
LIGHTWEIGHT
AL MIQUET (Huddersfield)
VERSUS
JIM BREAKS (Bradford)
British Lightweight Champion
COMMENTATOR Kent Walton
TELEVISION DIRECTION BY
PEMBROKE DUTTSON
ATV Network Presentation

3.15 News
The latest from the newsroom of ITN
FOLLOWED BY
A quick look around Wembley Stadium

3.24 Big Afternoon Out
See panel above

3.15 The Bugs Bunny Show
PRESENTS
High Diving Hare
This week's cartoon offering finds Bugs Bunny on the high-diving board, two faithful sheepdogs with problems, and Sylvester enduring further trouble with Tweetypie

3.45 News
The latest from the newsroom of ITN

2.40 The F.A. Cup Final
(First Half)
FROM
Preston North End
VERSUS
West Ham United
FROM
Wembley Stadium
The crown of the soccer season is presented with full uninterrupted coverage
COMMUNITY SINGING
CONDUCTED BY Frank Rea
ACCOMPANIED BY THE BAND OF THE SCOTS GUARDS
Organised by The Daily Express
COMMENTATORS

Gerry Loftus   Jimmy Hill
TELEVISION DIRECTION BY
STEPHEN WADE
Independent Television Presentation

3.45 Return to All-Star Wrestling

3.55 Return to the F.A. Cup Final
Preston North End
VERSUS
West Ham United
for the Second Half

4.50 Return to All-Star Wrestling
See pages 7-9

5.50 Thank Your Lucky Stars
INTRODUCED BY
BRIAN MATTHEW
Another hit parade of top pops brought to you by the stars of popping on tonight's show are
THE SHADOWS
ROY ORBISON
RONNIE CARROLL
EDEN KANE
BAND OF ANGELS
JAN BURNETTE
ME and THEM
TONY BROOK
JANICE NICHOLLS
heads a panel of teenagers who comment on the latest American releases in
Spin-a-Disc
GUEST DISC JOCKEY
ALAN FREEMAN
DESIGNED BY
BRIAN EATWELL
DIRECTED BY
PAT HBBINS
ABC Weekend Network Production

TV SATURDAY

BBC-1

10.35
THE FABRIC OF THE ATOM
An Introduction to Quantum Mechanics
by
Professor Philip Morrison
PROGRAMME 5
MATTER WAVES
Special equipment loaned by Professor Harry Messel
Troy, U.S.A.
Producer ALAN SLEATH
From the Royal College of Surgeons
† A BBC Educational broadcast
Repeated on Monday at 11.15 p.m.

11.5
PARLIAMO ITALIANO
Let's Speak Italian
A course of thirty lessons for beginners
20: PREPARANDO I BAGAGLI
Giulia takes over the packing for their holiday
WITH
MARIA LAZZI
ROBERTO CARDINALI
SERGIO GAZZARRINI
Introduced by
Arietta Reggio
Designed by
Charles Lawrence
DIRECTOR MADDALENA FAGANDINI
Produced by
PETER MONTAGNON
† A BBC Educational broadcast
Repeated on Thursday at 11.50 p.m.

11.25
NOTICE BOARD
Public Service announcements

11.30
GRANDSTAND
Including
F.A. CUP FINAL
GOLF
BOXING
ICE HOCKEY
See panel and page 7
Details of next week's Grandstand are shown on page 59

5.15
THE TELEGOONS
Peter Sellers
Harry Secombe
Spike Milligan
BBC Radio's world-famous Goons in a new puppet series for television
This week's adventure is
Lurgi Strikes Britain
Script by Spike Milligan
and ERIC SYKES
Television adaptation by
Maurice Wiltshire
Produced by
TONY YOUNG, of Grosvenor Films
for BBC-tv

† BBC recording

┌─ 11.30 to 5.15 ─┐
GRANDSTAND
Introduced by David Coleman

The F.A. Cup Final

PRESTON NORTH END v.
WEST HAM UNITED

BBC Outside Broadcast cameras bring you the whole match from the Empire Stadium, Wembley

11.30
Introduction and prospects from the pitch

11.45
The F.A. Cup Final—1963
Highlights of last year's match

1.25
How They Got There
Film of the finalists' outstanding matches on their progress to Wembley

2.0
Final Thoughts
by Danny Blanchflower. The captain of Spurs—reviewing side gives a player's-eye-view of the match and the occasion

2.10
Meet the Finalists
A close-up of the players in today's match

2.25 app.
Community Singing
conducted by Frank Rea

2.50
Presentation of the teams to
The Earl of Harewood

3.0 KICK-OFF

3.45
Marching display by The Massed Bands of the Brigade of Guards, under the direction of Major C. H. Jaeger, Mus.B., L.R.A.M., A.R.C.M., Director of Music, The Irish Guards Senior Director of Music, The Brigade of Guards

3.55, SECOND HALF

4.45
Presentation of the F.A. Cup and Medals by
The Earl of Harewood

4.50
Meet the Cup Winners
David Coleman talks to today's Cup contestants
Match Commentator: Kenneth Wolstenholme
Reports and summaries by Walley Barnes and Danny Blanchflower
Presented for television by Dennis Monger and A. P. Wilkinson

Golf
from Wentworth from 11.45
The final day's play in the
Martini Invitation Tournament
Commentators: Henry Longhurst, Bill Cox, Cliff Michelmore
Presented for television by Jones Lloyd at Alex Museum

Boxing
in America at 12.40
Frankie Narvaez (Puerto Rico)
v. Vincente Derado (Argentina)
Commentary: Alex Weeks
(According to the Colonna "Fight of the Week")

Ice Hockey
from Brighton at 1.5 and 1.40
Fife Flyers v. Wembley Lions
The final of the "Grandstand" tournament
Commentator: Alex Weeks
Presented for television by Peter Sole
Leeds Results and News Service at 5.5 app.
Presented by Alex Weeks. Editor: Cliff Morgan
(These show timings may be changed by events)

The two television networks duly issued their programme journals. ITV would only fire up their valves at Wembley at a rather conservative 2:40pm, unlike the BBC who would be back and forth from the stadium from 11:30am. Commentating for ITV was Gerry Loftus with comments by Jimmy Hill while Ken Wolstenholme and Wally Barnes provided the same service for the BBC.

ITV's obsession with Professional Wrestling would even see a bout squeezed in at half time; but I wonder how many viewers got into the cup final mood by watching, *"The Fabric of the Atom"* - at 10:35 am on BBC1?!

21   VALIANT, DEFEATED, RESPECTED

PRESTON NORTH END 2 WEST HAM UNITED 3
FA CUP FINAL 2/5/1964

Everybody reading this knows what the script of the FA Cup Final 1964 was. Despite bravely leading twice, North End finally succumbed in the final minute to lose 3-2.

It was only after the match that North End got some form of due praise from the press that had so cruelly written off their chances beforehand.

This précis of the match (overleaf) that supplemented a main report says it all; a southern reporter fairly noting North End's, *'sheer excellence of performance'* who *'by their unexpected aggressive resistance made this the match it was.'*

Of all the reports of the game this is perhaps the most concise that one could ever find, but it drives home hammer blows of admiration for North End's attempt to lift the trophy.

To be scrupulously fair, after the match was over the West Ham United players largely said the same. They paid due respect and probably hadn't foreseen such a difficult task when they kicked off.

North End lined up with: *Kelly, Ross, Smith, Lawton, Kendall, Wilson, Ashworth, Dawson, Spavin and Holden.*

After the usual formalities, the match started. Before long, a Spavin cross was hurriedly cleared by Moore, then Kendall demonstrated some neat 'northern' footwork that belied his years.

Second best since war

By JOHN THICKNESSE

TO get Preston's performance into perspective one had only to listen to those who have seen all the post-war Cup finals.

For sheer excellence of performance and prolonged excitement, they said, this put even Matthews's match—Blackpool v Bolton 1953 — into the shade. Only Manchester United's classic victory over Blackpool in 1948 took precedence.

In that they came twice from behind to win, West Ham's victory followed the pattern set by that United side led by Johnny Carey—but let there be no mistake that it was Preston, the Second Division underdogs, who by their unexpected aggressive resistance made this the match it was.

Lawton, their captain, Kendall, at 17, the youngest player ever to appear in a Cup Final, and Holden, veteran now of three, were among their great heroes.

Though West Ham eventually, I thought, just deserved their belated winner, they would have been far from disgraced had their adversaries emulated West Bromwich Albion's 1931 feat in winning the Cup from the Second Division.

Lawton picked up the ball in midfield and hurtled forward, with the North End fans roaring him on. His delightful through ball just evaded Ashworth and Dawson, the latter forcing Jim Standen in the West Ham goal into a desperate dive to whip the ball from under his feet. At the other end a centre by John Sissons, the 'Hammers' left winger, evaded Kelly's grasp and ran towards Geoff Hurst, but a timely intervention by Kendall killed off the threat.

Burkett, seemingly worried about his task for the day then sinned again, this time blatantly obstructing Wilson and receiving admonishment from referee and coal miner Arthur Holland. Nothing came of this free kick but it had been a very bright start for the team with 'no chance' of winning.

Indeed, around the ten minute mark, North End nosed ahead. Lawton's repeated raids forward were worrying West Ham, and from one such move Dawson found himself deep but with the ball. His shot was going wide, but Standen, harried and hustled by Spavin and Holden, failed to gather. The ball ran free, and Holden standing at the left post confidently turned it in before wheeling away in delight. The joy of both his team mates and the North End faithful was there for all to see.

Whether there was then a massive mental relax on the part of North End, perhaps we will never know — but around a minute later the recoiling Hammers were back on parity thanks to a lovely goal from 18 year old Sissons, who became the youngest player to score a goal in a FA Cup Final.

The winger seized the ball, raced through and cutting in drove a hard low shot past Kelly, the ball going in off the keepers left post. This time it was the East London roar that was audible for miles around.

Both teams settled down again and it was developing into an entertaining game.

Lawton was outstanding in his fetch and carry role and yet another defence splitting pass this time found Ashworth whose shot was deflected over the bar by Eddie Bovington's boot.

Kendall was also wowing the crowd with his performance. Displaying a confidence and maturity well beyond his years, he sold a dummy twice to Boyce to set off an attack that almost put North End back in the lead. His pass forward enabled Holden to cross for Dawson, but it was too long. Wilson retrieved the ball before it went out of play and lobbed the ball goalwards. It tantalisingly dropped on the wrong side of the crossbar and bounced to safety.

Singleton was holding firm against the menace of Johnny Byrne, the Hammer's England centre forward, but the forward did get a shot in that brought a full stretch save from Kelly.

Wilson, perhaps not seeing enough of the ball, got past Burkett again and centred - the ball hitting Moore in the chest area, bringing howls of 'handball!' from the hopeful North End fans.

Another fine run by Lawton also had the North End fans roaring. He launched a great shot which was deflected away for a corner.

Floated in by Wilson for Dawson, it was just too high but Holden standing behind controlled the ball and passed to Spavin on the edge of the box. His snap shot hit Ken Brown's arm bringing another huge cry from the North End fans, along with raised arms from the players - Brown's evasive action probably winning him the benefit of doubt from referee Holland.

Preston were not performing to the script provided during the previous week by the southern press. Their play was fresh, co-ordinated and causing the Hammers distinct and recurring problems.

None more so than in the 40th minute, when North End took the lead for the second time.

A shot by Kendall from outside the box ballooned off a defender for a corner on the right. As Wilson lined up to take the corner, the West Ham defenders were on walkabout; indeed their nemesis, Dawson was roaming free of Brown, his designated marker.

Courtesy Daily Mirror

Wilson launched his corner. As it approached, Standen came forward, slipped and retreated back to his line, but was now unable to cover his left. Dawson was powering in and Brown, picking him up late, slipped under him as the human wrecking ball leapt high to meet the ball.

Perfectly delivered, dropping bang on the six yard line in dead centre of goal, Wilson's corner was met full blast by Dawson who buried his header powerfully into the right hand side of the net (above).

What a great moment! A team of apparent no-hopers were about to take a 2-1 lead into half time. A tremendous performance.

All the problems lay at West Ham's door at this moment, but every game has two halves...

Ron Greenwood, who back then was an up and coming coach with ideas, had a problem. His midfield was being swamped and overrun by Preston and Lawton in particular. He had to come up with something - and fast.

He was frank with his players. He told them that North End were the best team and deserved to be in front. He also said that they had to go back out there and win the cup even if it killed them.

In an interview years later, Johnny Byrne explained,

"Ron told us that we were not finding each other coming out of defence and we had allowed Lawton and Spavin too much time and space in midfield, meaning play was passing 'Mooro' by - he hadn't done much at all in the first half.

"We had to do something to counter Lawton and Spavin. He told Eddie Bovington to make an impact and increase the tempo of the game, but also keep close to Spavin. Ronnie Boyce was told to pick up Lawton in a similar fashion."

Conversations about the game took place in the press box too – despite the fact that those 'expert' Fleet Street football pundits who had lambasted North End's chances during the previous week were also busy eating a huge dollop of humble pie.

Walter Pilkington of the Lancashire Evening Post recalled,

"By general consent in the press box, the football in this final was comparable with that when Spurs won the double, and when Manchester United beat Blackpool 4-2 in that memorable showpiece of 1948.
"Win or lose, North End had silenced all those critics who had thought of them in terms of a football 'working class' from the realm of caps and mufflers. The ridiculous sneering about 'fumbling and groveling' to success, aimed at a team that had stood third in Division Two for seven straight months had disappeared. North End had shown, to those who seldom saw them, undreamt mastery and cohesion, plus a flow of intelligent constructive ideas which recalled to old followers the traditions on which Preston football was built."

Well said Walter!

The second half began with Greenwood's plan in place. West Ham, as they had proved during their cup run were fighters. Thus, after only seven minutes of the second half, North End were in the unhappy position of having to do it all again after conceding an equalising goal.

Intercepting a ball destined for Byrne, Singleton's header went out for a corner. Peter Brabrook took the corner and it was just about met by Brown who headed it on deeper into the North End box where the ball was headed yet again from about ten yards out with some purpose by Hurst. The ball evaded Kelly's grasp and hit the crossbar. The 'keeper fell to the ground with the ball falling behind him in unison, seemingly catching him on the arm and squirming backwards just over the line.

Undeniably the game was turning, and Greenwood's plan was starting to work. Lawton and Spavin could hardly breathe now that Bovington and Boyce were up close and personal, and Moore was becoming far more influential.

Kelly saved a pile driver from Sissons, then a centre from John Bond was missed by Singleton enabling Hurst to direct a header goalwards - Kelly saving easily. Dawson then crashed a shot in after Ashworth had put him through, but Standen was in a good position to save.

With about 25 minutes of the game left, West Ham were dominating territory but North End were dangerous on the break.

Byrne flashed across a low centre which seemed to go too fast for everybody. Singleton, socks now rolled own, deflected a shot from Hurst for a corner when it seemed to be travelling goalwards. At the other end Wilson put Ashworth in but he miskicked completely. A drive by Wilson from a narrow angle was saved by Standen, then a rasping Bovington drive went just clear of the North End crossbar. A weaving run by Spavin promised great things, but he was bundled off the ball before he got in a shot.

The atmosphere was electric as both teams slugged it out on a pitch now taking an ever increasing toll.

With nine minutes left Kelly was left writhing in pain after a West Ham attack. The injury took some time to sort out, but eventually he resumed his position and was applauded appreciatively by the North End fans.

The beginning of the end of North End's FA Cup dream. West Ham equalise for the second time

Time was counting down fast; five minutes to go and Standen saved a 20 yard drive at full length, then he saved again, this time from Wilson. Lawton had a good chance but his shot went high and wide. Well into injury time with thoughts of extra time in everybody's mind, and the referee looking at his watch, West Ham struck.

Hurst passed wide to Brabrook who crossed for Boyce to head home on the run, leaving Kelly and his defence completely wrong footed. There were just seconds left...

The crowd rose to Moore as he received and lifted the Cup, and also to North End who filed up behind 'man of the match' Lawton to the Royal Box. Lawton's immediate and magnanimous post match comment to pitch reporter David Coleman was, *"The better team won."* There was certainly more than a touch of humility too when the sporting West Ham centre forward, John Byrne recalled his feelings just after the game.

"The noise from our fans was amazing. When we got back from the Royal Box we were all laughing. As I went on the pitch I spotted Nobby Lawton and couldn't help feeling sorry for him. He played out of his skin and had brought his side to within a hairs breadth of winning the cup."

Never mind the fact that they had lost the FA Cup Final or missed out on promotion to the Division One - North End were given a extraordinary welcome home when they arrived back in Preston, with tens of thousands of people turning out to line the teams route to the awaiting civic reception.

The Mayor told the crowd, *"They didn't win the FA Cup, but they won the admiration of the country."* Then, turning to the players alongside him said, *"You provided one of the greatest shows ever seen at Wembley. Thank you for the glory you have brought to the town of Preston."*

They had contributed hugely to a classic FA Cup Final and in the eyes of their faithful, this team was special. Special too, in the eyes of North End's most famous son, Tom Finney.

The Lancashire Evening Post 'Last Football' newspaper front page...

THE FAVOURITES GET A SHAKING
PRESTON WEAVE GLORIOUS PATTERNS
A HERO'S GREETING

by
Walter Pilkington
(Sports Editor)

WEMBLEY, on the occasion of its 36th FA Cup Final and the 83rd in a series which began, in the humblest manner imaginable, in 1871 had more of the traditional atmosphere of rivalry surrounding it than a number of these football "red letter" days of recent times.

That was because it was a clash between North and South partisans for the blue riband of the association and, more to the point, Lancashire v. London. The South, following the hobby of professional clubs, had to wait a long time to wrest the trophy from the grip of North and Midland clubs.

Magnificent

Vocal war

MOMENT OF DESPAIR FOLLOWS JOY

AS THEY PLAYED

THE CRITICS ARE SILENCED

Thrill after thrill

Centre of speed

Fervent response

Kelly to the rescue

Delightful patterns

Coventry club hat-trick in Blackpool race

Panel bowls

PROUD PRESTON SCORE

... and back page

It's painfully easy to spot the winners and the losers

Alex Dawson recalls :

"I once asked Tom Finney which was his favourite North End side out of all those he had played in and watched. He said, 'The team I liked best was the 1964 team.' I asked, 'Why?' and he replied, 'They were a team. You all had a job to do and you did it. You knocked some sense into the youngsters and then your mate Lawton joined. You had told the manager to get him and I told him too. I also told them to make him captain....."

Perhaps the last reflection of that day therefore should go to Nobby Lawton who recalled just before a special 40th Anniversary get together of the finalists :

"Do you know we hardly gave the ball away in that final, and as captain that made me so incredibly proud. The one thing I learned from Matt Busby at Manchester United was never to bother about the opposition, just prepare meticulously and concentrate on your own strengths. That's

what we did and Preston shocked West Ham. Bobby Moore told me afterwards he couldn't believe how well we held the ball and dominated the game until half-time. Of course the disappointment was immense to lose 3-2 after going ahead twice in the final, but we put on a great show and had a real go. I told the lads in the dressing room, they couldn't have done anything more and they'd done Preston proud."

Actually….that's *not* the last word about the 1964 FA Cup Final.

In 2004, the PNE Former Players Association held a special reunion to commemorate that great final. Not just for the Preston team; the hand of friendship was extended to the West Ham United players too. It was a great event, organised by Ian Rigby and George Ross.

I had made brief contact with George in late April 2016 at the start of this project, asking him if he could help fill in some gaps with my selection of games as he had seen them all unfold. I sent him a text promising to get back to him when I had a list of questions. The reply was typically helpful, and George was particularly looking forward to recalling both of the games against Leeds United in 1963/64.

Sadly and unbelievably, George is no longer with us, in a devasting year that has also seen us lose North End legends, Alan Spavin and Graham Hawkins.

I wanted to pay this North End 'Trojan' a tribute and with the very kind permission of Tony McDonald of *'Ex Magazine'* who report on all things from West Ham United's illustrious past, I feel that I can at least try.

George invited the *'Ex'* editorial team to the 2004 reunion so that they could report it back in words and pictures to their West Ham United readership.

The five page feature that follows is a superb and appreciative article by Tim Crane and pays due homage to George in the process. It is reprinted in full.

It's patently obvious that friendships were well and truly re-ignited that day...

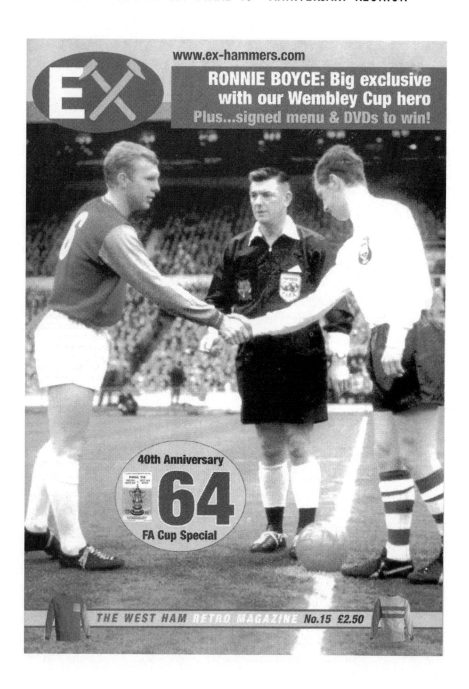

CUP FINAL REUNION

Preston did us proud

It shouldn't have been up to Preston to honour the players who beat them to win the Cup 40 years ago, but, as *Tim Crane* reports, PNE's Former Players' Association must take a well earned bow for putting on a great night in honour of both teams...

Well done to Preston North End's Former Players' Association! It was an absolutely tremendous effort to preserve the achievements of the past by staging one of the most memorable reunions ever.

What a great testament to the enduring greatness of the famous claret and blue five who made the trek from far and wide to join almost 200 other guests and play their part in respecting history and maintain the now fading traditions of West Ham United.

A big thank you to the great Sir Tom Finney for attending the event and elevating it from the stars to the very summit of all things good and worthwhile.

EDDIE BOV WON THE CUP!

A huge show of gratitude for Eddie Bovington, whose dry wit and watertight recollections made a real difference to the occasion. We have wasted no time in circulating the firmly held belief that, but for Eddie's injury (cramp in his right calf)

late on in the game, there would not have been enough time on the clock for Ronnie Boyce to win the match. Eddie Bovington did, indeed, win the Cup for West Ham!

Whether or not you subscribe to this view, you cannot deny the fact that Eddie 'The Bov' did, in the second half, limit the effectiveness of the highly influential Nobby Lawton. It was the successful application of a Greenwood strategy, which certainly played a big part in the outcome of the game. Eddie's rasping drive on the hour, which flew over the bar, could have made the margin of victory all the more decisive.

Hats off to Ken "Topper" Brown ("Don't ask me where that nickname came from," he says) for his jolly nature and desire to enjoy yesterday, today and tomorrow with a smile. His respect and admiration for both Bobby Moore and Budgie Byrne were all the more endearing given big Ken's senior status in the team. The sparkling banter surrounding his positioning when West Ham went behind for a second time courtesy of the prolific, Alex Dawson, still endures. Alex jokes that Ken claimed "foul" when the ball hit the net for Preston's second goal – despite being on his backside a few feet away!

Eddie Bovington and John Bond relax.

It should be noted that Ken can rightly claim the assist for Geoff Hurst's equaliser in the second half after his towering challenge made enough contact to paint the sky claret and blue once again.

Rumours that Ken still walks around with the base of the great old Cup, and wearing a claret and blue bowler hat, were sadly unsubstantiated! "Someone nicked it from me when I attended a 'do' at the Denmark Arms pub many years ago!" he explained.

A big pat on the back to John Bond for his lofty stature in West Ham's history and football at large, and for his comment that the 1964 achievement is at the very top of everything he has achieved in football. His comment that Ron Greenwood, who was usually reserved and tight lipped with praise, actually patted him on the back after the game falls into line

1964 FA CUP FINAL 40TH ANNIVERSARY REUNION

Still in demand, Ronnie Boyce pauses (with fag!) to sign autographs.

with the comments of former Hammer, Tony Scott, who felt, on the day, that John was man of the match.

In keeping with the big-hearted family man John has always been, it is his only regret that his son, Kevin (now Portsmouth coach), did not experience a trip to Wembley as a player.

A large slice of time and respect must be offered for the decency and honesty shown by Peter Brabrook who took time to pay his respects to Tom Finney, a man with whom he played alongside during the World Cup finals in 1958. As Pete (then of Chelsea) chatted to Sir Tom about them lining up on opposite wings against Russia in Sweden, it was one of the many powerful emotional moments oozing from within The Pines Hotel, Chorley, Lancashire on the weekend of May 8/9, 2004.

ENORMOUS THANKS

Peter talks from the heart and his appreciation of Ron Greenwood ("a tremendous coach"), to whom he owes enormous thanks for bringing him to West Ham and remaining patient with him, was sincerity defined. No one would question the fact that Greenwood's investment was returned with plenty of interest.

> "The fact that he has such comparisons to draw on gives a one-word answer to his standing in the annals of West Ham history – legend"

Then there is Ronnie Boyce. It is only fitting that he should pop up last of the West Ham contingent to fire the senses of his adoring fan base. The man who brought the whole of London's East End and beyond to the doors of Stratford Town Hall all those years ago was effortlessly laid back about his last minute header which continues to fuel the dream factory to this day.

His apology to the Preston players and fans for scoring the goal, which ended their dream, was fitting for an occasion defined by modesty and respect. He gave a clear answer to the two most frequently asked questions about his career. He does get asked about the strike at Maine Road as much as the FA Cup effort and he actually holds the European Cup Winners' Cup game as his greatest moment in the claret and blue. The fact that he has such comparisons to draw on gives a one-word answer to his standing in the annals of West Ham's history – legend.

Of the Preston boys, Alex Dawson, "The Black Prince", typified the abundance of character that graced the occasion and his enthusiastic anecdotes ensured a smile was never too far away. He is as warm and engaging now as he was deadly and prolific in his playing days.

The speeches from both Howard Kendall who, as a 17-

128

1964 FA CUP FINAL 40ᵀᴴ ANNIVERSARY REUNION

Above: Brownie gets closer to Alex Dawson this time than he did for their second goal! Below: Bondie signs a programme for Dave Wilson.

Proud Preston: Left to right: Tony Singleton, David Wilson, Howard Kendall, Nobby Lawton, George Ross, Alex Dawson. Doug Holden was unavailable at the time this was taken.

year-old lad, left boot prints of excellence on the hallowed Wembley turf, and Nobby Lawton, to whom he still refers to as "Skipper", brought wit and dignity to a hushed and enthralled audience of devotees. Video footage of the game reveals the match commentary of Kenneth Wolstenholme to be most passionate when describing the role of Howard Kendall: "He wasn't in the team on Monday and now he is sensationally having the game of his life!"

Nobby Lawton's captain's speech was full of praise and his assertion that "The better team won", was a statement from a true gentleman. It must be said that such a comment disguises the fact that the two teams had very little quality difference between them on the day.

His conversation at the bar with his Wembley adversary, Eddie Bovington, was a priceless moment as they shared their views. It was a noble gesture on Nobby's part to recognise the good work done by Eddie, particularly in the second half. Love was not lost but added to mutual respect and washed down with fine Lancashire ale.

Recognition of the tremendous effort made by centre-half, Tony Singleton, who flew from Los Angeles to team up once again with his old buddies, was shared by all and Tony's stunning 40-yard effort against Swansea in the semi-final was analysed at length once again. It was his one and only goal for the club!

Similarly, Doug Holden's opening goal at Wembley ensured a captive audience throughout the entire weekend and it was great to see Brian Godfrey, so instrumental in the early rounds of the great cup run, thankfully taking the time to meet up with his old mates. The evening benefited enormously as a result.

The performance of flying right-winger, Dave Wilson, in 1964 was eye-catching to say the least. He gave Jack Burkett a torrid time in the first half and posed a real threat to the Hammers. Even today he winces at some of the tackles and some would argue that Jack could have been the Kevin Moran of the 60s but for the leniency of Cup final referee, Arthur Holland.

I have chosen to leave George Ross as my final player reference because his tireless efforts, flawless organisation and keen willingness to provide comfort and assistance, from the first thought behind the reunion until the last swing of the hotel door, was nothing short of phenomenal. We praise his contribution and extend a warm and sincere show of appreciation to all who helped his cause.

George's comment about Jack Burkett promising to return Dave Wilson's kneecaps was inspired and heartily received. His decision to take time out of a very busy Sunday schedule (spent at Preston for their final game of the season), in order to play a part in a collection of video

129

1964 FA CUP FINAL 40TH ANNIVERSARY REUNION

interviews about the players' recollections of their Wembley experience, was typical of the Scotsman's selfless nature.

I couldn't possibly sign off this piece without mentioning the role played by the players' wives who provided colour and fun and an obvious talent for laughter and dancing throughout the entire evening. There was a charming concern for the welfare of past and present players they have met down the years. The sharing of memorable occasions and characters was perfectly placed in an atmosphere which thoroughly enhanced the well deserved title "Proud Preston" and "Happy Hammers".

As a West Ham fan, I have to confess that the respect for tradition, custom, history and achievement displayed by all related to the Preston North End Players' Association left me dismayed at our own club's failure to mark the anniversary of our first ever peace time Cup final victory. It is nothing short of shameful and I cannot think of one acceptable reason as to why a commemorative dinner was not organised with gusto.

Weakening traditions and a refusal to recognise great moments are dangerous habits to adopt. I have no choice but to place the club's behaviour on the scrap heap of decency along with the decision, this season, not to produce an official team photo for the first time in the club's history. I

Above: Ken Brown is proud to meet Sir Tom Finney, whom he played against only once for West Ham. Below: It's the turn of Peter Brabrook and Eddie Bov to chat with Sir Tom.

130

1964 FA CUP FINAL 40TH ANNIVERSARY REUNION

only hope they make amends with the European Cup Winners' Cup anniversary, the greatest night in the club's history, next year.

I prefer to look back at the riches afforded to us by the people of Preston and know that I am a richer man for knowing them.

End game: Eddie Bovington and Nobby Lawton – just after the Preston skipper paid tribute to the crucial marking role played by Eddie in the second half at Wembley.

THE WEST HAM RETRO MAGAZINE

The 1963/64 Preston North End first team squad – undeniably their best team of the decade and for some considerable time beyond...

23   CUE DEEPDALE

PRESTON NORTH END 2 WOLVERHAMPTON WANDERERS 2
DIVISION TWO 6/11/1965

On the world stage, this was the time when Ian Smith was poised to declare UDI in Rhodesia; in the UK, it was when Sunday afternoon football highlights finally arrived for the football fans in the North West of England!

The first game selected just happened to be the clash at Deepdale between two of the Football League's founder members, Preston North End and Wolverhampton Wanderers. The game certainly provided much excitement, was well received, and launched *'World of Soccer'* off to a flying start.

Wolves were flying near the top of Division Two, just behind Midland rivals Coventry City and looked likely to gain promotion. North End came into this game in indifferent form; their season stuttering. Wolves had the winning habit and the players to go with it.

Kelly was missing from the North End team after Injuring his shoulder at Grimsby in the League Cup tie. Unfortunately for him, he was also ruled out of the World Cup play off qualifier in Paris against Spain on the following Wednesday. North End lined up with :-

Barton, Ross, Smith, Lawton, Singleton, Kendall, Hannigan, Ashworth, Dawson, Spavin and Lee.

As anticipated, it was Wolves who set the pace. Quick, neat interplay with an obvious shoot-on-sight policy, the men in old gold were looking to strike early. Whippet-like winger Terry Wharton was the first to try his hand, slamming in a low drive bang on target which in the event, Barton saved quite easily.

At the other end, Dawson had soon discovered that his shadow was called Ron Flowers and he was going to be at the burly Scot's side all afternoon.

Wolves' continuing slick movement was getting the better of North End, making their hosts look pedestrian in comparison. Solid in defence too, Wolves really did look the part in the early exchanges.

David Wagstaffe, a terrifically quick winger, ran in from the left wing momentarily causing anxiety for North End players and fans alike when his header, en route to goal from a Wharton cross eluded Barton - but thankfully not Kendall - who was covering his keeper proficiently.

After the Wolves onslaught had settled, North End poked their noses out from their shelter and had a little spell of their own. A couple of shots flew in but off target, then Wolves escaped going behind only by the presence of mind of John Holsgrove, a most accomplished half back.

Lee crossed the ball in from the left and Dawson hooked a great right foot shot over the head of the advancing goalkeeper Dave McLaren. Seeing the possibility of the this situation early, Holsgrove was making his way to the goal line and deflected the ball sufficiently at full stretch to save a certain goal.

Spavin then put Ashworth through, but the big forward slipped and fell as he tried to gather the ball in his stride. It was to be a costly lapse, as Wolves gained control of the ball and motored forwards.

Every Wolves' forward pass was being placed in front of the attacker so that he ran onto the ball at pace as the defence backpedalled. It was Peter Knowles, a young and very accomplished striker, who set off in chase of a pass reaching it in his stride some 20 yards from the North End goal after leaving Kendall in his wake.

With just once glance upwards, he unleashed a terrific right footed drive that sailed into the top left hand corner of the North End net, with Barton still clawing fresh air as the net was bulging. It was Knowles' 15th goal of the season to date, and we were barely past Bonfire Night! The later overnight retirement of Knowles was subsequently well documented and he resolutely stands by his decision to leave football in 1969 to become a Jehovah's Witness. It has also to be noted he was an outstanding footballer, and could well have spent many years at the top.

North End stuck to their task well but the biggest threat to goal was the Wolves forward line. Knowles was either being extremely elusive or repeatedly being given too much space in which to operate as he tried his luck again from 20 yards out; this time the shot flying wide.

The sharp shooting tactics continued from the visitors and paid off once more as Wharton, picking up a pass near the corner of the penalty area shot instantly to beat Barton all ends up with a ground hugging drive.

Stunned, and now with the crowd on their back, North End soldiered on. Lawton was doing all he could in urging his men on continually, but too many passes and through balls went astray. Wrongly trying to compensate with over elaborate play that ended up down blind alleys, the crowd were frustrated still further.

Up front, Flowers was still marshalling Dawson well, and Ashworth was out of sorts thus North End's attack was limited and rather weak. The flanks looked North End's best option, where Lee in particular was having a good game.

There was a glimmer of hope just before half time when Ashworth had the chance to halve the deficit, but saw his shot tipped over the bar by McLaren for a corner. From the cross, Dawson launched himself into the thick of things, hampering McLaren's attempt to punch the ball way cleanly but Smith couldn't control his shot and it sailed over the bar.

A half time deficit of two goals would take some retrieving against a team as fluid as Wolves. Not a great TV debut so far for North End!

It was apparent after just a few minutes second half play that Jimmy Milne had attempted to address the first half North End 'issues' as there

1.55 World of Soccer

PRESENTS
Preston North End v.
Wolverhampton Wanderers
Edited highlights of the match
AT Deepdale
COMMENTATOR MARTIN LOCKE
TELEVISION DIRECTION BY
ANDY GULLEN

ARMCHAIR SOCCER

Television, and television football was a little complicated back in the 60's — as far as commercial tv was concerned.

Granada only broadcast to the north on Monday to Friday; the weekends were covered by the now defunct ABC. To add further confusion, some regions were served by ABC's rival ATV at weekends, and ATV was the company holding the commercial tv weekend football contract.

However, a deal was eventually struck (see right), between the two.

Initially, and rather surprisingly, ABC named the match they were to cover in the TV press, but this soon ceased after complaints from the clubs involved about drastically reduced attendances.

Preston North End v Wolverhampton Wanderers was the first game to be televised by ABC in their new venture.

The official attendance for the match was 15,971.

IT has taken four years of complicated negotiations. A constant series of meetings, discussions, protracted arguments.

The result is *World of Soccer* a completely new approach to televised football in the North — the regular screening of regional games.

It starts at 1.55 on Sunday afternoon, when ABC Television show highlights of the previous day's game between Preston North End and Wolverhampton Wanderers.

World of Soccer will be screening some of the most outstanding games to be played in the North. And *TV Times* will match these occasions with great behind-the-scenes features.

In the pages of *TV Times*, readers will be meeting some of the big names of soccer.

The first is Harry Johnston, ex-captain of Blackpool, who, in next week's issue, will be giving an inside view of the seaside team and its battle with West Bromwich Albion.

136

was now an visible *'let's get to work'* attitude about their play. Indeed, this was destined to be a classic *'game of two halves.'*

Lee, cutting in from the left, let fly with a hard drive that McLaren could only fend away back to the winger - the second attempt being deflected away for a corner.

Dawson then shot just wide from around 20 yards with McLaren well beaten. This surge of North End energy certainly raised the decibel level of the crowd, and they were shouting again as Hannigan - subdued throughout the first half by left back Bobby Thompson - sped past him and crossed dangerously only to see McLaren save well.

With Preston now dictating terms, Wolves with that two goal cushion, decided they were good enough to defend their way out of Deepdale and take home the points. They now resorted to the odd counter attack which the home defence were much more at ease with ... that was until Wharton broke free, drew Barton but then thankfully shot wide.

Lawton was rousing and chastising North End magnificently and the Wolves defence was being placed under increasing pressure. Lee was Lawton's main outlet of choice and he provided him with two more shooting opportunities that were taken but not converted. Ashworth and Dawson then both mistimed their headers after Hannigan had centred for them in quick succession.

The crowd were urging North End on, and sure enough the creaking Wolves defence did finally crack as North End pulled a goal back. Hannigan, now with the beating of Thompson on the right wing, hurtled down the line and delivered a terrific centre, curling slightly away from McLaren. It was almost a goal for Dawson as he leapt high, but the ball went over him and ran free to Lee stationed behind the action on the left. Without hesitation, the winger let fly for the far corner and was delighted to see the ball sail into the roof of the net.

What a strike, and what great television!

Preston's tails were now up, and they carried on ploughing forward with still 30 minutes left on the clock. Dawson directed a Ross centre with a header like a bullet from 15 yards that had McLaren stretching for his life, just managing to tip the ball away for a corner.

Wolves were certainly rattled. They had hardly seen beyond the half way line for nearly 20 minutes and still North End came forward. The calm, reassured defence of the first half had been replaced by siege mentality as they packed their area with every available player.

The crowd were right behind North End, and there was a sense that this game could still be won. The storming attacks continued apace, Lawton and Spavin reveling in midfield, pulling the strings. Kendall saw a shot go wide, then Lee was denied a carbon copy of his earlier goal by a brilliant one handed save from McLaren.

The excitement grew and grew, and with just over ten minutes left, North End thought they were on level terms as Lawton, stalking behind the action in the Wolves box, hammered in the resultant loose ball through the melee only to see Holsgrove stretch out a leg and clear off the line.The action was frantic, and back came North End for another try. A Dawson volley screamed in and hit McLaren's arm, followed by a tremendous drive by Hannigan that was goal bound but struck the back of a cowering defenders head and flew away for a corner.

There were just minutes left as North End were awarded a free kick on the edge of the Wolves box. Touched sideways to Kendall, the ball was drilled powerfully towards goal, and found the back of the net after taking a healthy glance off Joe Wilson that wrong footed everyone.

Kendall ran away arm aloft as the rest of the team chased him down. The crowd were finally sated and over the 90 minutes it was North End who had - in boxing parlance - a 'points win' after their continual pounding of the Wolves goal in a quite astonishing transformation.

Everyone was eager to watch the game on TV the following day.

'World of Soccer' duly played out its first edition and was reviewed thus in the Lancashire Evening Post,

"...as it was the excellent and well edited, coherent TV version showed North End in a most favourable light and endorsed what most of the crowd must have been thinking during this fine, fighting revival; that if *anything like comparable fire and determination had been forthcoming earlier, the Wolves would have been swamped"*

As it happened Wolves fell away in the promotion chase, (as did Coventry City), and both had to wait until the following season before gaining promotion.

It's still just about possible to see North End's first goal (above). Frank Lee (obscured by Ashworth) slams home a shot into the roof of the net.

24   SENSATIONAL DAWSON

PRESTON NORTH END 3 BOLTON WANDERERS 2
FA CUP 4TH ROUND REPLAY 14/2/1966

The wonderful FA Cup run of 1965/66 started with a 3-2 away win at The Valley over Charlton Athletic in the third round. Goals from wingers Ernie Hannigan and Frank Lee had put North End two up in the first 17 minutes, and despite a Singleton own goal North End led 3-1 at half time after Hannigan had struck again. The second half was seen out comfortably; so North End sat back to wait for Monday's fourth round draw.

Old adversaries Bolton Wanderers were the team paired with the Lilywhites, the tie to be played out at Burnden Park on February 12th.

Remarkably, this was the third year in succession that the Lancashire neighbours had been drawn to contest the FA Cup fourth round.

On a bitterly cold day in front of a crowd approaching 40,000, Wyn Davies put Bolton ahead in the ninth minute, flicking home a Brian Bromley pass to the home crowds' delight. However North End immediately rallied, and a cross from Godfrey was met with force by Dawson, whose header rattled the Bolton crossbar before goalkeeper Eddie Hopkinson even had time to think.

The Black Prince had been going through something of a lean goal scoring spell, but this was to end in the 14th minute. Smith floated a free kick towards the back of the Bolton goalmouth, where Dawson was

140

waiting. Leaping high once again he sent a tracer bullet header back across Hopkinson and into the top corner of the net.

Several 'oohs' and 'aahs' later, with North End resolutely clinging on, the tie was left undecided at the final whistle. Back to Deepdale came the two teams just 48 hours later, to contest in what would turn out to be a thrilling match.

With first choice North End goalkeeper Kelly still unavailable with a damaged elbow, John Barton continued his run as his stand-in; the team named being the same as for the match at Burnden Park:-

Barton, Ross, Smith, Lawton, Singleton, Kendall, Hannigan, Godfrey, Dawson, Spavin, Lee.

Two Lancashire clubs now vying for the right to host Tottenham Hotspur in the fifth round in front of 31,558 fans gave value for money in a rousing, non-stop cup tie.

This was to be a match in which the enthusiasts in the crowd would go home nursing hoarse throats, such was the amount of incident that occurred in this 'derby' that needed shouting about. The game had a bit of everything - top class goals, tension, fluctuating fortunes, thrills and spills.

As in the confrontations of previous seasons, both teams played in their change strips.

It became clear soon after kick off when Hannigan was kicked into the air by full back Bolton Roy Hartle what the visitors tactics were going to be. An initial gasp from the crowd as they witnessed the blatant misdemeanour turned into boos and jeers very quickly, and thus Bolton had set the tone in which they wanted to operate.

Initially, North End protested to the referee about the persistent ruggedness, but then decided to 'look after themselves' - not being disposed to take the rough stuff lying down.

It wasn't as though the strong arm tactics gained Bolton any advantage; certainly by the 12th minute it hadn't!

That's when Godfrey, smoothly accelerating forward through the middle of the pitch, fed Hannigan on the right wing with a well directed headed pass. With the noisy anticipation of the crowd pushing him along, the tricky Scot moved forward at pace and launched a centre into the Bolton box.

The ball beautifully swerved over and around the lanky Bolton centre half John Napier's desperate leap and fell just outside the six yard box, whereupon Dawson launched himself forward like a diving nuclear submarine to meet the ball and head low with such skill and direction that Hopkinson couldn't prevent the inevitable. It was a sensational goal, and how the crowd jumped and cheered.

The play was peppered by admonishments from the referee to both teams, but the hard, ruthless streak that Bolton were displaying seemed to be no accident. North End had been dragged into a rough house contest; perhaps that was the Wanderers' aim.

Two 'Lees' were on show, one for each team. Both were christened 'Francis,' both attended the same school, both were in the same class. Both played in the same school football and cricket teams. They were not related. Preston's Lee eventually called himself 'Frank,' to distinguish the pair apart.

It was Francis Lee of Bolton who was causing the North End defence some trouble. Quick and more than happy to throw himself around and play to the crowd, his interplay with Gordon Taylor was superb.

On one such occasion, he was put through with only Barton to beat but shot well wide, the crowd reminding him of his miss with loud jeers.

Two minutes later, and those North End jeers had turned to groans as opportunist Lee put Bolton on level terms.

Taylor floated in a corner, and defender Dave Hatton, on a forward sortie, headed the ball sideways to the waiting Lee, in a little square of land all of his own in front of goal. Requiring no second invitation, Lee pounced and buried the ball into the net past Barton.

Desperately trying to rally, North End were being hoofed in all directions

Diving into the Lead

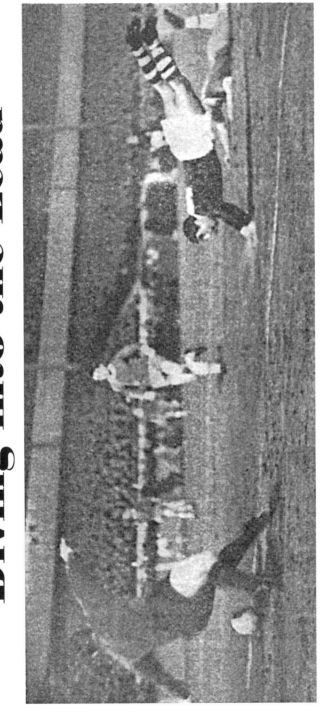

Fantastic, fantastic Alex Dawson! The North End centre forward scores the first

by this unyielding Bolton team. Indeed, at one point the crowd had only just stopped yelling their opinions at yet another dreadful challenge on Godfrey, when Spavin was delivered an awful jab to the groin by a Bolton boot and had to be carried off for attention.

The crowd increased their decibel level to new heights as the referee did nothing more than lecture Hartle.

A behind the goal view of the moment the ball flashes in for North End's opening goal

A quick North End thrust up the pitch after play resumed for the second half was roared on by the faithful. A lovely passing movement involving Spavin, Godfrey and Hannigan ended when the winger drilled the ball wide of Hopkinson's right post.

Worse was quickly to follow. Much worse. Bolton attacked and a crisp and deceptively powerful drive by Davies wasn't collected cleanly by Barton. The ball span behind him long enough for the oncoming Davies, following through with a run, to nip behind the embarrassed keeper and prod the ball into the unguarded North End net.

The Bolton fans shouted and sang, but didn't celebrate any harder than Davies. He went crazy; even delirious. Leaping high several times with one arm raised aloft in the prevailing manner of the times he ran hither and dither. Never had a forward been so gleeful.

What happened next was quite unbelievable. Less than two minutes later - and who knows, perhaps still very over-exhilarated – Davies did the very same arm raised salute when Smith floated a free kick into the Bolton penalty area and handled as Hopkinson was ready to collect the ball.

Now it was the North End fans in loud delirium as the referee halted play and instantly pointed firmly at the penalty spot. Davies sunk to his knees. He eventually walked slowly back and out of the area without looking up, clearly finding it hard to quantify his moment of 'brain freeze.'

Godfrey placed the ball firmly on the spot, retreated and ran in to calmly place a hard, accurate shot into the upper right hand corner. North End were back on level terms and now ramped up the tempo.

Godfrey makes no mistake from the penalty spot to put North End level

The ball was being swiftly played wide by Lawton and Spavin as the attacks were launched. Hannigan had now seemingly developed a hopping technique to evade the lunging tackles of the previous hour and was making inroads down the right.

As if one penalty were not enough, Bolton kindly threw in another for good measure on 68 minutes.

Hannigan, hugging the right touchline, cut inwards and skipped around Syd Farrimond. Moving swiftly forward, he also beat Hartle dashing across the penalty area to stop him regardless of the consequences, and was unceremoniously scythed down. It was a quite ridiculous lunge that effectively cost Bolton the match.

Godfrey was nonchalant once more when placing the ball and even when he had to retrace his steps at the referees behest and start again. He chose the same route as for his earlier strike and Hopkinson was completely beaten by the hard rising shot.

Cue more deafening noise from the home crowd whose loyalties were now even more partisan after the uncompromising tactics meted out by the visitors.

Kendall was called upon to smartly cut out a dangerous ball crossing the North End area en-route to Francis Lee, and was again to the forefront a few minutes later when a back pass was over hit and nearly evaded the clutches of a relieved Barton.

The last 15 minutes saw few goal attempts and North End held out with icy detachment to earn the plum home tie with Spurs.

Every player on the field gave his utmost. There was a lot of wasted energy spent by Bolton however, whose preoccupation with stopping North End playing rather than utilising their own talented performers cost them dearly. The risks involved in such a strategy proved enormous and it hardly endeared the huge Deepdale crowd when those obvious and prolonged 'man or ball' tactics were continually employed, resulting in free kicks and injuries galore.

Looking forward, North End manager Jimmy Milne commented, *"Spurs? It will be 11 against 11 as far as we are concerned. Believe me, it won't be any harder than this one."*

Poetic justice for Preston or poetic retribution for Bolton? Whatever your view was, for those 90 minutes of intense football excitement these two clubs were anything but neighbourly rivals!

25   HIS NAME WAS ERNIE...

PRESTON NORTH END 2 TOTTENHAM HOTSPUR 1
FA CUP 5TH ROUND 5/3/1966

The North End fans amongst the 36,792 present for this game will never forget it.

First thing to note was that Deepdale was bathed in sunshine on a lovely spring day and looked fantastic. It certainly did to me as a nine year old - my eyes agog at the number of people inside the ground.

My dad, unable to make the pilgrimage that day, had got me a ticket and another for a friend slightly older than myself.

The tickets were for the Pavilion Paddock, and we went through the turnstiles at the corner next to the Town End. There was then a large bank of concrete steps to negotiate which brought you out just at the top of the standing area of the terrace.

Once there, we couldn't see a thing the crowd was so big...and, from a nine year old's perspective, tall! I can recall us both tiptoeing and jumping to try and glimpse the pitch - but that wasn't going to last long!

A voice said to me, *"Owt in your pockets lad?"* I shook my head at the person I thought had spoken to me. Within an instant I was hoisted aloft and then started a downwards journey above the heads of the spectators present with the same voice shouting behind me, *"One coming down, lads."*

Over the heads of the assembled throng I descended, and by now worrying that I had lost contact with my mate who my dad had told me to stick close to.I needn't have worried; he was about 20 rows of fans behind me coming in the same direction! Finally placed down behind the concrete barrier and half time scoreboard at the front, I was quickly joined by my mate again. What an unbelievable experience it had been; and thanks to the kindness of the crowd I could now see everything that would unfold.

A huge roar went up as both teams emerged from the tunnel. Spurs were in a change kit of black shirts with white shorts and socks, which I still think even all those years later, looked rather elegant. All the Spurs star players I had seen on TV week in, week out were there right in front of me. Dave Mackay, Pat Jennings, Jimmy Greaves, Alan Gilzean, Alan Mullery - the list was endless for this 'Bank of England' team..

North End lined up with:-

Kelly, Ross, Smith, Lawton, Singleton, Kendall, Hannigan, Godfrey, Dawson, Spavin, Lee.

Spurs fans were dotted around everywhere too, indeed around 8,000 had made the journey north, and were very vocal.

Cliff Jones, Spurs' Welsh international left winger had not recovered from a bruised shoulder in time and this meant that manager Bill Nicholson had to slightly reshuffle his pack. He decided that Jimmy Greaves would don the number 11 shirt, with utility player Eddie Clayton replacing Greaves at inside right.

The game kicked off to another huge roar, with Spurs attacking the Spion Kop. What had been a quite remarkable day for me so far, then took a seeming turn for the worst. With barely a couple of minutes gone, Spurs took the lead, after a move that seemed effortless to them. The ball was passed across the field to feet in an incisive, deliberate fashion, and eventually launched into the North End box and over Kelly's head from the left by Frank Saul.

Jimmy Robertson, dashing forward, met the ball at the junction of the six yard box and the goal line and headed back across the face of the

North End goal. Waiting at the opposite post - of course - was the one and only Greaves, who side footed home the bouncing ball without any hesitation.

Just the Spurs fans were audible at this point, but at least North End had virtually the whole game left to wipe out this debit - assuming of course that they could gain some sort of foothold in the game.

Lawton got North End firing and was simply superb in his fetch, carry and distribute role. Kendall and Spavin also started to ask a few questions of the Spurs midfield and defence. Despite this, the visitors had an air of superiority about their play and with time on the ball were dealing with anything that the increasingly rumbustious North End could throw at them.

Lee and Hannigan were becoming prominent, and Lee went on a superb mazy run, swerving past a couple of defenders before shooting just wide. Hannigan then put Jennings under pressure a couple of times after beating full back Cyril Knowles down the right.

Spurs refused to buckle, and nothing seemed to be an effort as they glided forward after any failed North End attack. The crowd were being treated to a classic contest of a very talented aloof team trying to keep their wholehearted opponents at arm's length.

The game was increasing in pace, thanks largely to Lawton's constant urging in midfield. Ross then boomed forward down the right and fired in a good cross, but Jennings, once again the cool, calm and collected epitome of a classy goalkeeper, plucked the ball out of the air without any problem.

Dawson found some room in the box, but mishit his shot when challenged - even so the visible relief on Mackay's face told us that they knew all about Dawson and what he was capable of. Lee and Hannigan were crossing at every opportunity, perhaps sensing that Laurie Brown at centre half would rarely have dealt with a 'beast' such as Dawson before. In terms of possession, North End were well in front but still searching for the key to unlock the Londoners' defence.

So, when the reward for their all out efforts finally arrived, it was no more than they deserved. Ross, out on the right, launched an accurate cross into the Spurs area towards the back post. Dawson, lurking in the vicinity and with the chance of a goal beckoning, dashed forward from Brown leaping high above him sending a firm looping header back past

Dawson puts North End level against Spurs – as only he could

and above the rooted Jennings into the far corner. It was due reward for sheer strength and persistence. With the crowd in noisy delight, Godfrey ran into the net to collect the ball and hoof it high into the air. Dawson meanwhile, had wheeled away towards the corner flag area running very close to where I stood with his arms raised high in celebration.

As you can imagine, this left a lifelong impression with me.

The man was huge; almost gladiatorial. His legs were very thick but muscular and his upper body seemed almost square and undoubtedly packed with great strength.

He was joined by Spavin, Lawton and I think Lee, with captain Lawton shouting loudly into their ears above the crowd noise as they made their way back.

Wow! It's just as fantastic recalling it now as it was seeing it back then.

Play recommenced, and North End kept up the tempo, urged on by the crowd at every opportunity. Spurs were certainly pinned back as North End dominated this period of play. A good move down the left fell to grief when Spavin took too long deliberating what to do; Phil Beal neatly reliving him of possession.

In a rare excursion forward, Greaves managed to get a shot on target only to see Kelly pat it down with ease.

Towards the end of the half, Dawson became entangled with Jennings and play was halted as the centre forward received prolonged treatment for an injured right leg. The referee finally drew the first half to a close, North End leaving the field at half time to rousing cheers, and were well worth parity. They had controlled the latter part of the first half and had given the visitors plenty to think about over the break.

After a few minutes play in the second half, it was obvious that Dawson was playing with some real discomfort. Any dash of over five yards and a distinct limp became apparent in his movement. His frequent little forays wide had ceased and he was restricting himself to the middle of the pitch. With no bench bristling with replacements as in present day football, Dawson and North End just had to grin and bear it.

As the half progressed, Spurs seemed to be in the process of 'shutting up shop' – just happy to hold North End at 1-1 rather than go for the knock-out blow. If their strategy was to draw, they were certainly going the right way about it.

Their attacks were scarce and, despite North End being very much on the front foot, with the top class defence that Spurs possessed, why wouldn't they feel confident of holding a team who stood a mere 14th in Division Two?

North End's undoing was their finishing, with Godfrey and the now hampered Dawson wasting hard earned openings by firing blanks at Jennings.

Lawton, Spavin and Kendall went on providing the opportunities; possession - and indeed intent - was running high in North End's favour. The crowd were urging North End on, especially when Lawton gained control of the ball and moved forward.

On the hour, North End attacked again - but this time delivering a stunning blow.

Lee, who had been something of a revelation on the left wing, passed infield to Spavin around 30 yards out from the Spurs goal. Moving forward and approaching the Spurs box, the midfielder seemed undecided as to what to do. Opting to go it alone, he moved into the Spurs box and fired an unforgiving rising drive at goal that Jennings, at full stretch, couldn't hold - parrying the ball directly into the path of the unmarked Hannigan, following up in true goal poachers fashion.

The winger, being watched apparently from the Pavilion Stand by a plethora of scouts and managers, plunged the ball into the back of the net with the outside of his right boot. This goal, and his general performance in front of those scrutineers must have advanced his value by many multiples.

At the time of course, I hadn't experienced anything quite so exciting 'live', and I just didn't want the game to finish!

So, with roughly 30 minutes left, Spurs were suddenly panic stricken as 'Plan A' had to be quickly torn up. They certainly raised their game at this point, but North End withstood gamely all the increased activity in front of their goal.

Greaves looped a shot in after a quick move down the left, but Kelly was equal to it. Then Gilzean, with his back to goal and stood just inside the North End box, trapped a firmly hit through ball from Mullery at his feet and quickly turned. Obviously not expecting Singleton to be stood just six inches behind him, the Scottish international cannoned back through the air to land on his backside, leaving the North Ender to calmly play the ball wide to Smith.

Above: Just before the axe fell on Spurs' cup hopes – Jennings can't hold Spavin's shot and palms the ball directly into Hannigan's path.

This brought cheers from the home fans, as they, like the Spurs players could see the tie going North End's way.

They weren't home and dry yet though, and with about 15 minutes to go, Deepdale held its collective breath as a defining Spurs raid unfolded.

Saul, approaching the right hand side of North End's penalty area and about to be converged upon by Smith Lawton and Kendall, moved a step to his left and threaded a pass through them aiming for Greaves on the opposite side of the box.

Ross, stood in the path of the ball near the penalty spot had the chance to curtail the move instantly but delivered a most uncharacteristic 'air swing' of the right leg, allowing the ball through to find its intended recipient.

This was it. This was the moment. Greaves with the ball now under control, was one on one with Kelly just ten yards out to the left of goal.

Kelly came forward from his goal line a few yards to narrow the angle and Greaves, instead of striking the ball with some degree of power back across the goalkeeper, opted instead to try and bend it past him at the near post. His left foot shot was saved well by Kelly, the ball hitting his chest and dropping to the floor as he dived to his right. Ross, atoning for his error of a few seconds before ran between the striker and goalkeeper to offer Kelly protection in re-gathering the ball. Phew!

More good movement from Hannigan put Godfrey in the clear but running out of space as the ball hurried along. He managed to manufacture a shot from a very acute angle which surprised Jennings who had obviously expected the ball to run out of play for a goal kick. Remarkably the shot appeared goal bound until Jennings changed direction and flopped on the ball just inches from the line.

With the fans whistling, and Mackay's arms waving about all over the place Spurs lumped the ball up the middle of the pitch once more to Gilzean but it was cleared yet again and shortly afterwards the referee blew for the end of the game.

That night, Match of the Day featured the Wolves v Manchester United cup tie, but in his summary of the day's results at the end of the broadcast, Kenneth Wolstenholme duly acknowledged North End's performance as '*the result of the day*' - fair praise indeed!

We had discovered over the years that school dinner times were just long enough to cram in the FA Cup draw, and one of the football daft fraternity had brought his brothers portable radio along in his satchel. Whether his brother actually knew was open to debate, but we all gathered around the in a massive circle to listen and some I recall were counting down the teams on their fingers.

It must have been hilarious to watch 20 or so wise old nine year olds listening intently, getting more and more animated. "That's six," shouted one and then my pal chimed up, "I've not heard Man Utd yet..."

He was still uttering these words as the voice in London said, "Preston North End will play...Manchester United."

There was an instant of silence. Then utter joy accompanied by lots of noise and leaping about like we had all just scored a goal. "I'm going on. Are you?" was the instant new question that was answered in the affirmative by one and all. Knock out Spurs on Saturday and draw United at home on Monday – unbelievable!

It meant such an awful lot when we were just nine years old...

North End – United 'plum' at Deepdale

The LEP back page headline on March 7th 1966. Wow!

Bob Bond's summary of the very memorable day in '66 when North End beat the mighty Tottenham Hotspur

*Bob's book, '**With A Sketchbook At The Match'** features many illustrations and tales of Deepdale and North End in the 1950's, when he was 'but a lad...'*

26   "DAWSON...A GOAL!"

PRESTON NORTH END I MANCHESTER UNITED I
FA CUP 6TH ROUND 26/3/1966

The fortnight following that almighty win against Tottenham Hotspur had seen FA Cup expectation build up in the town to the same level as a couple of years before when North End went all the way to Wembley.

North End were hosting Manchester United in the quarter-finals. It was still sinking in.

Everybody was talking about it. Tickets were like gold dust, but once again my dad managed to get hold of a ticket for my friend and myself for the Pavilion Paddock.

The day was wet and dreary, and I recall going very early, as we wanted to be able to get to the front without being 'airlifted' into place again, kind as the gesture was!

Once in, we made our way to the area where we had watched the Spurs game...an early touch of superstition perhaps...and waited for the ground to fill up. It certainly did that. Looking back, I find it impossible to believe that the Spurs attendance could have been topped - but it was - as a further 1,100 fans were squeezed in to take the official attendance to 37,876.

Well before kick off the seemed to be a 'kerfuffle' at the back of the Kop. Then the police and St. John Ambulance attendants could be seen

Interest in the game was such that the Lancashire Evening Post launched a 'Souvenir Edition' newspaper

struggling upwards through the crowd congestion towards the area of concern. Crowds were not segregated back then, but this wasn't a case of animosity. At the back of the Kop was a concrete wall which held back the crowd from a stairwell that served that specific area. With so many fans in the ground it was hard to be sure, but it looked like the wall had disappeared. This was soon confirmed by the crowd around us. The next half hour or so saw a procession of injured spectators of all ages and sizes brought down to pitch side and led away for medical attention. They were taken to Preston Royal Infirmary, fortunately quite close to the Deepdale ground.

An official statement later said the of 26 that were injured, 11 were treated at the PRI for head injuries, broken ribs, pelvic injuries and shock, but no patient was considered to be in a 'serious' condition.

Meanwhile, Jimmy Milne stuck with the tried and trusted team that had closed Spurs out so well in the previous round:-

Kelly, Ross, Smith, Lawton, Singleton, Kendall, Hannigan, Godfrey, Dawson, Spavin, Lee.

It is interesting to note both teams performances since the previous round. North End had drawn at home to Huddersfield Town and away at Crystal Palace and won at Bolton Wanderers. Manchester United had won 5-1 in the European Cup at Benfica (a match that certainly confirmed George Best as 'world class') lost away at Chelsea, and won at home to Arsenal.

The rain had stopped by the time United ran out first in their red shirts to loud cheers from their many fans inside Deepdale. It was hard not to concede a soft spot for them; they were rapidly re-gathering the ground that they had lost when almost wiped out just a decade before following the Munich disaster. Their 'team' performance in Benfica had been sensational.

Lawton led North End out to cheers - and a few United boos - and it was United who eventually kicked off towards the Town End, remarkably aiming for a fifth consecutive FA Cup semi final appearance.

Early exchanges were brisk - Bobby Charlton taking the ball off Lawton's toe in midfield, and putting Denis Law in for a shot that was a very good rugby league conversion. At the other end, Dawson challenged and the ball fell to Lee, whose attempted shot at goal was strangled at birth by the advancing Harry Gregg; the ball cannoning away for a corner.

This had the home fans cheering loudly, and even louder when Dawson's header from the corner appeared to strike the base of the post before being booted up field by the grateful Tony Dunne.

United hit back, moving swiftly through midfield. Charlton, already asserting his authority, swung a lovely through ball for winger John Connelly to latch on to, but after rounding Ross, sliced his effort out of play for a goal kick.

Another through ball by Charlton, this time for David Herd, saw the ex-Arsenal forward shoot well wide.

From Kelly's long goal kick, Dawson with back to goal, headed down neatly for Spavin to stroke a lovely first time ball wide to Godfrey in the inside left position. Stiles was left trailing as Godfrey pushed the ball forward and ran, but his centre found nobody in attendance bar Gregg, who collected with ease.

Law then collected the ball wide on the right, just in the North End half. Seeing George Best move down centre field at pace he passed diagonally, superbly threading the ball between Kendall and Singleton. Best collected the ball at full throttle, looked up and saw only the advancing Kelly between him and the 'onion bag.'

Shrieks of terror from the younger North End followers could be heard as Best fired in his shot, but Kelly somehow managed to block the ball and Preston breathed again.

Indeed, United were settling into a business-like and dangerous looking team, varying the starting point of their attacks astutely. Their football flowed with neat short passes; the longer version coming exclusively from the boot of Charlton. The North End 'schemers' were being kept very quiet.

North End broke this spell of United dominance when Lee set off a move with a throw back to Spavin from near the left hand corner flag.

The midfielder's cross beat the leaps of both Dawson and Foulkes, but fortuitously fell to Hannigan stood directly behind in a good position. Unfortunately he couldn't control the ball which bounced off his hip and then the advancing Gregg's body, falling eventually to the recovering Foulkes who hoofed it away.

Back came United, and Herd was put in the clear from a high pass and leaving Ross in his trail and thundered in a terrific angled shot which Kelly plucked out of the air in brilliant and spectacular fashion.

Next it was Pat Crerand's turn to be put through, but before he could receive the pass, Kendall had read the situation perfectly and intercepted with some panache. Just before half time, North End broke the deadlock and took the lead.

Lee wide on the left around halfway, passed inside to Spavin who took the ball forward some 15 yards before passing to Godfrey, creating space at the corner of the penalty area. His quick turn and cross caught United on their heels somewhat, with Foulkes for once caught well away from Dawson.

Spavin by this time had progressed unmarked into the penalty area, and Dawson cushioned his header directly into his path. It seemed to hold up on the surface for a split second - long enough for Foulkes to bear down on Spavin, who quite remarkably didn't panic at all.

He simply passed it back instantly to Dawson taking Foulkes out of the game, leaving the Black Prince one-on-one with Gregg, seven yards out. There was only one winner, the ball hitting the net before Gregg hit the ground. There was an explosion of sound when the ball screamed in. Dawson was mobbed by his teammates and, arriving back last at the centre circle he faced them all, clenching his fist.

The goal is quite remarkable in that the classy and unselfish Spavin never once looked forward at goal; his only intention ever was to get Dawson in a position to score.

It was described thus by Ken Wolstenholme on Match of the Day, *"Lee into Spavin….Godfrey….Dawson – a lovely chance for Spavin….DAWSON ….a goal! Preston have scored!*

By the time the players have got back for the kick off he rightly observes, *"….the fantastic thing was the way the ball was passed and re-passed in front of the Manchester United goal, which shows how much the Manchester United defence was ripped apart."*

So, a team that embarrassed Benfica 5-1 in Portugal had seen their own defence *'ripped apart'* by North End just 17 days later…the same commentator at both matches by the way!

Half time terrace talk was all about being just 45 minutes away from the semi finals. Two blokes right behind me were discussing it, (maybe father and son), the younger of the two waxing lyrical about North End's semi final prospects. The older one was pouring the cold water jug of reality all over this optimism, summing up his rebuttal with words I can still recall it pretty well,*"…and then there's the bloody tickets. After the time I've spent queuing here for tickets over the past few years I deserve some sort of long service award, and what's more in future they should be delivered to me by hand on a silver bloody platter."*

A moment to savour... Alex Dawson slams North End ahead in the FA Cup quarter final at Deepdale

The obtaining of match tickets for a big North End game was certainly a burning issue at the time...

The second half commenced and after the early exchanges, it didn't take long for United to draw level - just three minutes in fact. A pass infield from the right by Law to Charlton was crisply forwarded to Best in centre field, around ten yards from North End's penalty area.

Approaching Singleton, Best gave him a 'shimmy' and slotted the ball forward and to the right, directly into Herd's path. With only Kelly advancing from his goal line in front of him, Herd took the ball in his stride and slotted home.

David Herd slides the ball under Kelly for Manchester United's equaliser

Lots of younger United fans then ran onto the pitch to mob their idols. Lawton, who had spent the entire first half with his shirt out of his shorts, was now safely tucked in all round and trying desperately to lift his troops. He was very vocal with an attitude to admire.

Spavin, approaching the box fed Lee with the ball on the left. The winger turned nicely to lose his marker Shay Brennan, but saw his shot deflected for a corner by Law, chasing back to assist the Irish defender.

The corner was cleared and soon United were advancing again.

Charlton, with acres of room in the middle of the field, curled a glorious ball out to the left for Connelly to run onto. His cross cleared the leaping Law by at least a few feet, but the energetic Scot retrieved the situation by keeping the ball in play and passing backwards to Brennan. He clipped the ball sideways to Crerand who seemingly walked through the North End back line as though they didn't exist.

By now waltzing his way towards the byline, Crerand's cross was cleared for a corner before one of Charlton, Connelly or Herd could lay a boot on it.

United were certainly on top and had Preston hearts in mouths when they had appeared to have scored a second.

A Kelly drop kick was headed back towards Best, who controlled the ball after it passed Kendall. Instantly running between Singleton and Kendall, he was in the clear and running down centre field towards the North End penalty box.

Law appeared in space from nowhere to his right, but instead he took the ball right to the edge of the box attracting three defenders. Spotting Herd now in space to his left, Best delivered a pass from under his feet perfectly to him who slammed home the ball past Kelly from around 12 yards.

The referee disallowed the goal straight away for offside, but it must have been marginal. Best was roving all over the pitch and proving a real thorn in North End's side.

North End's midfield were being denied the ball, and for now at least, it was one way traffic. Connelly fed the ball inside for Charlton, who struck a long curling pass aimed for Law to run onto. Law couldn't cope with both Kendall's attendance and the awkward bounce of the ball however, and cheekily handled the ball to his advantage and ran on. It was spotted immediately by the linesman but so typical of Law to play up to the linesman with a huge smile on his face, arguing he had been robbed.

The next big incident probably decided the outcome of this game. A clearance by Smith just inside his own half on the left, turned into a superb through ball to the lively Godfrey by virtue of it eluding the outstretched leg of Crerand.

Taking the ball under control as he sped towards the box, Nobby Stiles was moving across towards him. As they were about to meet, Godfrey pushed the ball past Stiles and, at the same moment, Stiles pushed his right leg through Godfrey's left to terminate any possibility of the North Ender progressing.

Godfrey went face down in the mud at some speed and it was a little while before he regained his feet after extensive work and cajoling by trainer, Walter Crook. While this was happening Crerand and Stiles seemed to be standing over Godfrey accusing him of play acting, and to his credit Charlton pushed them both aside, appearing to tell them to back off.

Stiles was eventually booked for what was a quite disgraceful challenge.

With loud boos still ringing around the ground, Spavin took the free kick but it was cleared without any trouble.

North End then embarked on a spell of dominance. Hannigan went on a tricky run infield from the right wing but as he was lining his shot up on the edge of the penalty area, he was heavily tackled and dropped to the ground. 'Play-on' was the referees signal, much to the annoyance of the North End fans.

Brennan did provide a free kick though, running through the back of Lee as he was about to receive a throw.

The cross into the penalty area went through to Dunne on the left side who released Best instantly, but the move fell away when Singleton intercepted his pass.

Best appeared again menacingly homing in, this time from the right wing but he was robbed and relieved of the ball by the twinkle toed Lee who set off down North End's left advancing a good 60 yards before passing infield to Spavin.

The game was now becoming bogged down in midfield with both teams determined not to concede an inch.

Best had to leave the field after seemingly falling awkwardly after 78 minutes. Although the concept of a substitute had begun it was only available in league games, so United would have ten men for the remainder of the match – or so it appeared. Best actually returned after five minutes of 'magic sponge' treatment.

A Gregg drop kick was returned down the right wing by Ross into the path of Godfrey, who crossed into the box where Dawson met the ball cleanly with his head, but without the power needed to get past Gregg, diving to save on his goal line.

As time was ticking away, it was left to Kendall to save North End's bacon and give them the replay they so richly deserved.

Law moved down North End's right and set up Herd to centre the ball. The cross descended over the six yard line, with Kelly deciding to run from his line and punch it clear from the heads of Best and Connelly. This he did but with little power, and he found himself in no man's land with Law set to pounce.

The Scot did just that, sending the ball past Kelly's vainly outstretched arm, en-route for the right corner. Fortunately, Kendall had returned to observe proceedings from underneath the North End cross bar and headed brilliantly clear to the cheers of the North End faithful.

There was still time for Best to win another corner for United after being stopped in his tracks by Ross. As Kelly leapt to catch the ball, he seemed to fall awkwardly and despite the attention of the trainer, Walter Crook - running onto the pitch as the final whistle blew - had to be assisted off the pitch, limping badly.

In the event, North End would be without Kelly for the replay which took place at Old Trafford, with reserve goalkeeper John Barton standing in.

North End goalkeeper Alan Kelly
is helped from the pitch by both
trainers after damaging his
ankle

Preston North End's injured goalkeeper Alan Kelly,
seen here being helped off the Deepdale pitch by the
rival club's trainers with his opposite number, Harry
Gregg, sympathetically concerned, is a doubtful
starter for Wednesday's replay with a sprained
ankle. An X-ray photograph today did not show
any broken bone.

27   HEARTBREAK

MANCHESTER UNITED 3 PRESTON NORTH END 1
FA CUP 6TH ROUND REPLAY 30/3/1966

North End named the same team for the Old Trafford replay, apart from Barton replacing Kelly, who was by now nursing a sprained and swollen ankle.

The first half began with North End under early pressure, but batting back any serious attempts on their goal without any undue difficulties.

As the half wore on, the home fans in the bumper 60,433 crowd were becoming slightly agitated at United's seemingly over cautious approach to this game, especially as the visitors had the temerity to launch the odd raid of their own.

It was United who broke the deadlock on the half hour - thanks to being presented with the scoring opportunity by the visiting defence - the only delay to the inevitable outcome being the time it took Kendall and Barton to gift wrap the opportunity.

Barton, who in all fairness had proved himself to be a more than able deputy for Kelly, was stooping and about to collect a cross unhindered in his hands. Kendall, for some inexplicable reason decided to put his boot through the ball at the same instant, dislodging the ball and watching it roll directly into the path of goal poacher supreme Denis Law, who profited instantly with a finish demonstrating distinctly more composure than that of the hapless pair of Kendall and Barton.

Despite the fresh, enthusiastic roars from the Old Trafford faithful, their heroes couldn't break through the North End defence again before the interval; the visitors ears probably still ringing from the words Lawton yelled out as they trudged back to the halfway line after going one behind.

With United being nothing as fluent as at Deepdale, Jimmy Milne's half time talk must have centered around going forward with more purpose. I say 'must have' because that is exactly what was apparent as the second half built.

It was on one such forward sortie, with around 20 minutes left, that Kendall was put in the clear by a Spavin pass, threaded through centre field. Making progress towards goal, his shot was deflected for a corner on the left.

Singleton had taken an interest and jogged forward, planting himself just outside the six yard box. Lee's corner was delivered perfectly, and the aforementioned Singleton moved forward and soared superbly above the defence to rocket his header into the roof of the net.

It was a classic header, classically executed.

The congratulations over, North End built on their success and looked the better outfit. There was no suggestion of sitting back and playing for extra time, and the team actually won applause from the home crowd as they continued to move forward.

Dawson had been completely in old team mate Bill Foulkes' pocket all night, but his partner Godfrey nearly dispatched North

Tony Singleton equalises for North End
and throws the quarter final into the melting pot with 20 minutes to go

End into orbit when he had a snap shot at goal cleared off the line by Dunne, who hoofed the ball clear with Gregg completely beaten and looking on in vain.

With 88 minutes gone, it was certainly looking like extra time though, with no further chances falling for either team. That's when Kendall conceded a corner, arguably when he had no need to - but by the same token obviously having every confidence in the North End defence.

John Aston swung the ball into the now densely populated North End penalty area, and Barton made his move towards the ball. He got to it - just about - but because of the clamour punched weakly, the ball finding a surprised Foulkes. His first instinct was to toe-poke the ball forward any old how, and after travelling through a ruck of players, it fortuitously fell to that man Law, who helped it along the way by slotting it into the net.

A last gasp winner - what could be worse for the North End fans so full of hope just 30 seconds before? How about a final minute back-to-back United goal to completely put the tin hat on any wildly remote ideas of a North End comeback? Unfortunately, that was the script pre-written for this match.

As North End were trying to hurry the ball forward it fell to Aston wide on the left. He dashed forward and his cross was met by David Herd who headed goalwards, the bouncing ball being scooped home by John Connelly from close range.

The final 20 minutes of this match had been breathtaking, and far from being disgraced, North End had put up a splendid fight, until they fatally faltered when on top. *The Manchester Evening News* mused, *"..although United scored first through Denis Law, Tony Singleton equalised and Preston were looking the more impressive side...extra time was snatched away from Preston when they looked likely to finish the stronger team."*

There was much honour in defeat for the heartbroken North End, but it was United who would go forward meet Everton at Burnden Park on April 23rd - for that fifth consecutive FA Cup semi final.

United's last-gasp goals sink proud Preston

TWO-MINUTE
CUP TRIUMPH

Courtesy United Review
North End are hustled out of the FA Cup quarter final at Old Trafford

Inset: Law hits the ball home to give United the lead in the 88th minute
Main picture: Connelly hooks the ball in for United's third a minute later

Gallant, but luckless Preston

Late goals put
United in
semi-final

171

28   A STITCH IN TIME...

PRESTON NORTH END 9 CARDIFF CITY 0
DIVISION TWO   7/5/1966

So, after another season of FA Cup heartache - not to mention lower mid table league form, North End reached the last game of the 1965/66 campaign. It was to be a sunny but bizarre spring day; the game played out in front of the lowest home gate of the season - just 10,018.

North End lined up with:-

Kelly, Ross, Smith, Lawton, Singleton, Kendall, Hannigan, Godfrey, Greenhalgh, Spavin, Lee.

They were entertaining Cardiff City, who had been bouncing around the base of the division for months.

The Welshmen's defence was known to be over generous, and this was the day when it was proven beyond all doubt. It was so generous that it enabled Preston to rack up their biggest win of the century!

With their faint relegation worries banished a week before, North End relaxed and played with such unshackled style and abandon that they racked up an amazing nine goals without reply.

Settling down into attacking mode from the word go, it took North End just 35 seconds to almost push their noses in front, when Lawton robbed a defender without any resistance and saw his snap shot just roll wide of the post.

We didn't have long to wait - just another nine minutes in fact - to see Hannigan convert the first of his hat trick, after a lovely through ball from Lawton, who could hardly believe the amount of room he was being allowed to move in. Cardiff goalkeeper Dilwyn John dived through the air bravely, but couldn't lay a hand on Hannigan's angled shot as it flew past his right hand and into the Town End net.

As the waves of North End attacks increased in number - and along with them a string of near misses around the Cardiff City goal - Spavin was coming to the fore and was wreaking havoc.

Passing long, short or intermediate, he was sensational and with his partner in crime Lawton, carried the onslaught to the visitors with persistence and precision.

After 20 minutes, Lawton hooked the ball home from around six yards out with the Cardiff defence statuesque following good work by Godfrey.

The one way traffic continued and the crowd were left shaking their heads in astonishment as Brian Greenhalgh headed home from close range following a Hannigan corner, perfectly placing the ball between both Cardiff full backs stood on the goal line after 27 minutes.

Despite the ironic cheers from the home fans, Cardiff actually managed a couple of shots on goal themselves with Barrie Hole's piledriver the best of them, just flying past the angle of post and bar.

Then on 38 minutes normal service was resumed as Spavin threaded a beautiful ball through the Cardiff defence, eluding everyone bar Hannigan who cracked the ball in mercilessly from just around ten yards out.

As if four wasn't enough, Hannigan duly completed his first half hat trick on the stroke of half time. Rising high - and helpfully completely unmarked - to meet a cross from the right, he headed home in classic fashion. There we had it; North End 5-0 up by half time and playing fluent, attacking football without a care in the world. Applauded loudly from the pitch, the team deserved every bit of praise for such an unrelenting performance.

Oh, dear, what can the matter be?

What a way to end the season—1, 2, 3, 4, 5, 6, 7, 8, 9 goals

WIN OF CENTURY

Preston revel in the sun

IT WAS a day for dreaming and nostalgia in the sun at Deepdale as Preston scored their biggest win this century and Welsh international Brian Godfrey claimed one of the fastest hat-tricks on record in the 71st, 73rd and 78th minutes.

There was nostalgia for the good days of Preston at this hint of the old mastery and subtleties. And dreams that Preston could soon become a First Division outfit again with any kind of consistency next season.

BLISTERING

Until a few days ago both clubs were haunted with relegation. But only Cardiff seemed to be suffering from a hangover from a league career.

Not until the 12th minute did the Welshmen put any menace into attacks with Bird driving inches over the bar and Lewis using a blistering shot lift over the edge.

By then Preston were three ahead and Cardiff's defence was rubber-legged, chasing shadows because of a peculiar attitude that seemed to begin close making at a dizzy phase.

Certainly I have not seen a more haphazard defensive display this season in any division, not Godfrey nor Preston's Scottish star Ernie Hannigan will grumble about that as they garnered two hat-tricks. Hannigan's in the first half for Preston to turn round five ahead and already assured of their biggest win of the season.

With only one previous home victory win since December 6, Preston moaned as though determined to make up lost ground.

From the opening seconds Lawton showed just how hamstrung the Cardiff defence was by easily mopping the defenders and creating his shot but, by the wrong side of the post.

TREMENDOUS

After eight minutes the goal burst started. A clever pass by Lawton enabled Hannigan to score with a tremendous angled drive.

His hat-trick was completed in the 28th and 44th minutes with goals by Lawton (29 minutes) and Greenhalgh (27 minutes) sandwiched in between.

After this first half hammering Cardiff held out—until Godfrey struck.

His hat-trick was sparked off in a successful penalty, after Lee had been brought down by young Summerhayes.

Then, with eight minutes to go, lumbering centre forward Greenhalgh set the crowd howling for ten when he slipped a Lee centre past John.

ONE: A big effort, but John couldn't stop Hannigan's shot.

TWO: Nobby Lawton (4) scores his goal.

THREE: Centre forward Brian Greenhalgh heads in the first of his two.

FOUR: Hannigan hits his second.

FIVE: Hannigan's hat-trick.

SIX: A penalty is given away and Godfrey nets the first of his three.

SEVEN: It's Godfrey again.

EIGHT: And again.

NINE: And finally Greenhalgh wraps it all up.

Express Newspapers

174

The same unyielding domination continued in the second half, albeit with a little more input from the visitors. The action was cranked up in the last 20 minutes however, during which North End almost doubled the half time lead.

Lee, who had been quite superb on the left wing all afternoon, was felled in the box by Cardiff wing half David Summerhayes - Godfrey calmly slotting the penalty home to score his first of the afternoon. Within six minutes he had scored twice more to surely score one of the quickest hat tricks in Football League history!

With City's yawning defensive gaps screaming to be penetrated, North End obliged and Lawton saw to it that Godfrey could amble towards goal with no defenders in his vicinity and slot home past hapless the Cardiff goalkeeper to notch his second on 74 minutes.

This made the score 7-0, and immediately the younger fans started chanting, "We want eight!"

Godfrey duly met their demand in the 76th minute, once again Lawton setting North End's very own Welshman off trotting alone through the Cardiff box, for another one-on-one with John. A neat clip was enough to claim his hat trick and take the North End tally to eight. "We want nine!" was the immediate demand from the fans...

Six minutes later, Lee provided a lovely cross for Greenhalgh to run onto from the left and slide the ball home with a right foot jab. Up went the cry, "We want ten!"

The visitors were bamboozled and run off their feet to the point of demoralisation, and the game finished as one sided as it had started. It was an utter rout for Cardiff, whose only consolation was that their hosts were kind enough not to covert at least four other great opportunities.

29   REVENGE

QUEENS PARK RANGERS 1 PRESTON NORTH END 3
FA CUP 3RD ROUND   27/1/1968

To really enjoy and appreciate this win against the odds, we must rewind exactly by one week to 20/1/68 to briefly revisit what was in effect, a dress rehearsal for this FA Cup tie.

The same teams played at the very same venue but in a Division Two fixture. QPR led the table, while North End sat a dismal third from bottom, having gained just three points from a possible 18 in their last nine matches.

They had also experienced something of a refit in the previous few months; Archie Gemmill, Derek Temple, Ray Charnley, Ken Knighton and Graham Hawkins had all arrived; Hawkins in fact signing on from Wolves just seven days previously.

QPR meanwhile, were the up and coming London team. Momentum had obviously continued apace after winning the League Cup at Wembley along with promotion from Division Three in the previous season. They also had a young Rodney Marsh in their ranks - always a bonus - and the press were displaying a fawning adoration for him week in, week out.

It all went wrong for North End early. Hawkins lasted just five minutes on his debut, pulling a muscle and was unable to carry on. Marsh (of course) then scored immediately and the pressure was heaped on and on by Rangers. Considering the re-arranging that North End had to do on the hoof, keeping Rangers at bay until the 78th minute when Marsh finally added his second was something of a feather in their cap. The game duly ended 2-0, as millions had no doubt forecast on their Pools coupon - 'a home banker.'

The southern press had a field day. As an example the match report in the London edition of the *Daily Express* states that, *"If Preston improve sufficiently to win on Saturday, (the forthcoming FA Cup tie), Rangers fans will demand a dope test."*

Rather prophetic words as it turned out!

Just a few weeks before, Bobby Seith had been appointed as 'Team Manager' with Jimmy Milne 'moving upstairs' until the official handover at the end of the season. After learning that as well as the new signing Hawkins, Knighton and Ross would also be unfit for the cup tie, Seith set to work on a blueprint; working title - *'Seith's Super Sucker Punch of 68.'*

Scheming to exploit weaknesses in the Rangers defence was one thing; stopping Marsh was another. Simple! Seith literally glued Jim Smith to his back like a limpet and took it from there.

It went ever so well...

The patched up North End line up was:-

Kelly, Patrick, Ritchie, McNab, Cranston, Smith, Lee, Lyall, Charnley, Gemmill and Temple.

Smith politely reminded Marsh of his presence a few moments into the match by, let's say, *'not letting Marsh settle on the ball.'*

The tone had been set; Marsh didn't fancy it and North End could see the possibilities. This game was to be much more of an even contest than the previous encounter and quite soon the visitors had created a half chance from a McNab free kick - George Lyall shooting just wide from Charnley's downward header.

Rangers came back, and Ian Morgan went close with a header that flew inches over the bar.

North End were noticeably breaking quickly on the counter and Temple was caught just offside from a lovely through ball from McNab. It was a a big improvement, and the subtle changes could be seen.

McNab was featuring more in midfield than defence and was playing well. He set Lee off down the left who cut the ball back to Ritchie, but the left back blazed over the bar from 20 yards. More creativity from McNab saw Lee put in again, only to be badly fouled by Bobby Keetch before he could pass to Lyall, running into space.

Home confidence, both on and off the field was wavering; in contrast the North End fans dotted in the crowd couldn't quite believe what a turnaround this was. They certainly began to believe as Gemmill picked up speed and powered down the touchline as only he could.

With the QPR back line haring back into position, he fired a hard low cross towards the Rangers penalty area. Temple cleverly stepped over the ball, allowing it through directly behind to Charnley who now had the space and time to fire the ball home past former England goalkeeper Ron Springett. It was a superbly worked and well deserved goal for the Lilywhites.

Savouring of the goal had to be done quickly, as within a few moments, Roger Morgan crossed the ball into the North End box where it was met on the run by Rangers captain Mike Keen, who buried a fierce header beyond Kelly and into the net.

Ah well, back to square one! Well...not quite. North End were edging this game, especially with Smith's continual presence tangling Marsh up in knots whenever he received the ball.

Temple then shot just over from a Gemmill pass, and these two were working well together. Gemmill in particular, was amazing. On a very heavy and muddy surface, the little Scot's energy levels knew no bounds, and towards the end of the half the Rangers defenders were struggling to keep up with him.

Half time came, and North End could hold their heads high as they went for their brew and pep talk.

Rangers came out all guns blazing - for a little while anyway. Alan Wilks almost plotted his way through the North End defence, before Bert Patrick hoofed the ball well clear of any danger. A mention here too for Bill Cranston, in the side covering for Hawkins. He was dominant, alert and quite superb at dealing with anything the raiding Rangers forwards threw at him.

The game then settled back into the pattern of the first half, Marsh still completely ineffective, North End absorbing the rest of what QPR threw at them and then countering with the intelligent running of Gemmill, Temple and Charnley. Temple then went down complaining of a leg injury which developed into a long stoppage; the home crowd loudly complaining that Seith was relaying messages on to his players via the trainer. Maybe he was...!

Marsh was becoming increasingly agitated by Smith's attention and at one stage pushed and shoved at the half back, conceding a free kick to add to his frustration. Not five minutes later, the doyen of West London football randomly lashed out and felled Lee with an awful challenge, resulting in an instant booking from the referee.

Noticeable after that incident was the geeing up of each other by the North End team who probably sensed that Rangers were on the brink and were there for the taking.

Springett ran out from his goal to kick the ball clear before Gemmill reached it, but turned his back and started jogging back to his line before seeing that the ball had gone straight to Lyall who had dispatched it back instantly on the half volley. Shrieks and howls from the crowd saw the keeper turn around just in time, and he watched it go wide of the post to his immense relief.

North End were now playing the high line game for a change and the action was firmly in the Rangers half, and it was Lyall again, this time breezing across a defender who saw his slickly turned shot pushed around the post by the fully outstretched Springett.

Then, at last, it happened.

Charnley, who had been more than a handful for Rangers all afternoon, latched onto a through ball. Taking time to control the ball and beat off a challenge from Keetch, he confidently slipped the ball past the approaching Springett to put North End ahead.

It was a superbly taken goal and how the players celebrated.

As before, Rangers launched an immediate salvo, but they had a touch of desperation in their play and lacked their usual cohesion. North End meanwhile, had the air of winners about them, competent and unruffled in defence, dangerous in attack.

Courtesy of QPR FC
McNab and Ritchie calmly see the ball out of play to end another QPR attack

Kelly was called upon to save brilliantly from a Wilks shot lashed in from the left and shortly afterwards a downwards header from Keen bounced just past the North End post - the Rangers captain then flinging a piece of turf to the ground demonstrating his sheer frustration.

There wasn't long to see out now, and the faint whistles of the handful of North End fans could be heard in the now virtually silent Loftus Road.

It was then that Gemmill chose to put the thickest coat of icing ever on a North End victory cake when, well into injury time he stormed forward yet again, beating four tired defenders on a wonderful mazy run before hammering the ball home to the sheer and utter delight of his team mates and those faithful travelling fans.

Game, set and match - and a goal worthy of Tom Finney to seal it! What a day and what a result - considering North End had been disrespectfully lumped with Barrow and Bournemouth as 500/1 outsiders by the 'bookies' before this match.

It was a wonderful win. Seith deserved credit, as did his players for executing and sticking to the plan of continually targeting a couple of QPR defensive areas and Rodney Marsh, so very well.

Following the fourth round cup draw on Monday lunchtime, North End had to wait for FA Cup giants Tottenham Hotspur and Manchester United to settle their third round replay.

United went out at White Hart Lane... and so did North End by 3-1. The tie was televised on Match of the Day and showcased another gallant effort by the Lilywhites, as well as another wonderful FA Cup goal from Charnley.

30   HERO

PRESTON NORTH END 3 HUDDERSFIELD TOWN 1
DIVISION 2   23/3/1968

The selection of this North End game from the Sixties would have fit just as comfortably under 'unmemorable matches' had it not been for the magical performance of a certain Willie Irvine which richly elevated its status.

Irvine had been a surprise transfer deadline day purchase from Burnley on March 15th 1968. He was a superb striker, and ended his 'Clarets' playing career with the phenomenal record of 78 Division One (Premier League) goals in just 124 outings and 97 goals in all his 144 appearances.

Those statistics are amazing, and stand alongside the best from his, and for that matter anybody else's generation.

His arrival at Deepdale for £45,000 caused quite a stir at school, as Burnley were in Division One nobody had ever seen him play, but had read his name regularly in 'goal scorer capitals' in the Football Post.

Arbitration from the teacher was sought because one lad was insistent that the new recruit's surname was pronounced 'Higher-vine.' All was well, once the vagaries of English pronunciation were explained to him.

I was in my last year at 'Junior School' back then, and little did I know that the comfortable school life I enjoyed so much would soon be shattered in early September by the move up to Secondary education.

Up to July '68, everything seemed simple. We all got on with the teacher, who made lessons humorous and enjoyable. He gave the eldest pupils in the school some latitude which wasn't abused and everybody wanted to attend; we were the big fish in the small pond. Then came Colditz...!

Irvine made his debut at Ipswich Town on 16th March, and as was standard procedure away from home during that awful season, North End received a pummeling - losing 4-0.

After Irvine had played, scored and assisted North End to beat Aston Villa on the following Monday night at Deepdale, a few of us arranged to meet up at North End outside the club shop to see Irvine play against Huddersfield Town on Saturday afternoon. It was to be a great decision by a bunch of 11 year old football know-alls!

This was an important fixture for both teams, as Huddersfield Town were struggling too.

The bottom end of Division Two looked like this - North End gleaning just five league points since their FA Cup heroics at Loftus Road two months previously.

Pos		P	W	D	L	F	A	Pts
15	*Derby County*	33	11	7	15	58	62	29
16	*Aston Villa*	32	13	3	16	42	47	29
17	*Huddersfield Town*	32	9	10	13	34	48	28
18	*Bristol City*	32	9	9	14	31	47	27
19	*Hull City*	32	8	10	14	43	57	26
20	**Preston North End**	**31**	**8**	**7**	**16**	**32**	**54**	**23**
21	*Plymouth Argyle*	31	7	7	17	29	55	21
22	*Rotherham United*	31	6	9	16	32	63	21

The weather was awful. Constant rain had been falling all morning, and with a strong wind blowing, the four of us decided to go through the Town End turnstiles, safe in the knowledge that at least we could keep dry all afternoon.

Out the teams came for the 'kick-in' and within no time those immaculately white North End socks were splattered with muddy spray from a pitch that seemed as though it was about to submerge. Every time Irvine tapped the ball to Kelly he was cheered by a huge throng of kids, (including us), firmly planted behind the goal. He was already a hero.

Injuries, both long and short term had beset North End in the previous few weeks, so Seith played the following fit and available XI :-

Kelly, Patrick, Ritchie, Smith, Cranston, McNab, Temple, Irvine, Charnley, Knighton, Gemmill.

The match kicked off and was soon competing with the weather for the 'dreariest event of the day award.' It was plain to see why these two teams were struggling. The football lacked quality, the passing was atrocious and there seemed to be nobody from either side willing to get a grip of this game and make things happen.

In the players' defence it has to be said that the pitch was largely the problem; but it was so frustrating - all we wanted to do was see Willie Irvine score for North End!

If there was a 'better' team, it was Huddersfield. Paul Aimson, roving all over the place up front for the visitors did actually get the ball in the North End net, but was called for offside by the linesman.

North End were kicking towards the Kop, and had the strong wind behind them, but their attacks were so sporadic that the forwards were receiving no service at all. The home fans were moaning and groaning.

A broad yell of frustration from a bloke behind us that you just never forget occurred around then, *"Seith, wi this lot playin why spend money on Ervin when thi could have gorr-owd ovva Magic Robot for nowt?!"*

That caused a real laugh; intimating that Irvine was stationary due to pitiful North End approach play, (the *'Magic Robot'* was a general knowledge toy for children that somehow answered questions by swiveling and pointing (but not physically moving) to the right answer.

However, the tide turned on the half hour when Knighton blasted a tremendous long shot at the Kop goal out of the blue. The Huddersfield keeper, John Oldfield, could only parry the fierce drive into the path of Irvine who slotted the ball home without any drama to give North End a surprise and rather undeserved lead.

For us kids, this was bliss! The brand new Deepdale hero had now bagged his second goal in three starts - brilliant!

The excitement eventually died down and the game returned to its sepulchral state. Huddersfield ventured forward once or twice, and a free kick struck from the edge of the North End penalty area by winger Brian Hill breached the North End wall, but pulled up stone dead in the goalmouth mud bath to the ironic cheers of the home fans.

Just before half time, North End managed to control the ball long enough to enable Temple to float in a pin point cross for Irvine, who headed just wide.

With even heavier rain now falling as North End started the second half, it was a surprise to see North End moving a lot more briskly than in the first half, and looking a lot more likely.

Irvine won an early free kick which Patrick curled in towards the box, finding the head of Charnley whose neat flick went to waste as nobody was alert enough to seize the opportunity.

Panic then occurred in the North End box, when Patrick woefully under hit a back pass to Kelly which Aimson intercepted. Having navigated his way through the mud around Kelly, the centre forward then shot into the side netting with the goal at his mercy. Much relief all round for North End as Aimson sank to knees in disbelief.

A miss like that can prove costly, as was to be seen moments later.

Gemmill cut in from the left wing and drilled a shot in at Oldfield who turned it round the post for a corner. 'Go-Go' Gemmill as his name suggests, ran in and picked the ball up and then ran to the corner flag.

His corner was floated over neatly, straight to McNab who controlled it perfectly. He pushed it onto Irvine, who although surrounded by defenders, eagerly slammed it past Oldfield on the turn. It hit the net with some force and had all of us jumping around screaming for our new hero!

Huddersfield, to their credit, still came forward even though they must have felt demoralised. David Shaw made good progress down the wing and was just about to start cutting in towards the North End box when he was stopped dead by a Cranston tackle.

At the other end, Charnley latched onto a through ball and hit a snap shot from outside the box that Oldfield did well to tip over the bar. Meanwhile Shaw was still wandering around limping after his 'pressing of the flesh' with Cranston and had to be substituted; Ray Mielczarek running on to play in the mud.

Indeed it was Cranston who popped up again, sliding a lovely long pass through to Gemmill. Collecting the ball on the move, the young Scot centred promptly for Charnley, who couldn't quite leap high enough to make contact with the ball. However, lurking behind him was the redoubtable Irvine, waiting to unceremoniously blast the ball into the net past defender Billy Legge and the diving Oldfield from 12 yards - right in front of us again!

Into orbit we all went! This man was fantastic!

Looking back, Irvine's persistence was superb. His anticipation of where the ball was going to land or appear was outstanding. No wonder he held such a brilliant goal scoring record. That doggedness nearly earned him a fourth goal shortly afterwards, when he forced his way past three defenders only to be robbed at the last moment by Oldfield.

Ritchie carved his way through the mud and launched a shot from fully 30 yards that won appreciative applause from the crowd, then Temple had a good shot held under the bar by the keeper - but despite North

End's continued raids, Town scored a consolation goal five minutes from time through substitute Mielczarek, who converted a John Archer cross from the left.

The pitch was invaded at the final whistle as the younger fans wanted to swamp Irvine, who at that particular moment, meant everything to them. Yes, I ran on the pitch too with my friends but we didn't get close enough to pat him on the back. Irvine was a class act - a master - and his ability in front of goal proved it beyond all doubt.

Top: Irvine slams home his second goal after turning on a sixpence

Bottom: Irvine completes his hat trick , hammering the ball past Oldfield

Willie Irvine needed the assistance of a police escort from the pitch after the Huddersfield Town game. His post deadline day presence was one of the main reasons North End retained Division Two status in 1967/68.

Bob Bond featured Willie Irvine's hat-trick against Huddersfield Town as one of the Irishman's 'moments' of his career in a series called 'Star Strip' that featured in 'Football Monthly.' This piece appeared in the December 1968 issue.

31   FOREST FELLED

PRESTON NORTH END 3 NOTTINGHAM FOREST 0
FA CUP 3RD ROUND   4/1/1969

There was little to cheer about as 20,008 of us gathered at a gloomy Deepdale early in the new year of 1969. As well as the dismal weather that hung over the famous old ground, there was the much more depressing question of North End's current form - just three points gained from a possible 14 in the last seven league games. Little did we know how exciting the next few weeks would be!

The first weekend of the new year was traditionally FA Cup Third Round day, and North End had been paired with Nottingham Forest - tucked into lower mid table safety in Division One.

Arriving at the ground to find a collectable gold fronted version of the official programme on sale, it appeared that at least the club were trying to whip up enthusiasm and make this an 'escapist' day for the weary home fans on yet another pilgrimage; the hope being that the team too could cast aside their league form and enjoy themselves.

On a heavy surface, the North End team was:-

Kelly, Ross, McNab, Spark, Cranston, Heppolette, Temple, Knighton, Irvine, Ingram and Lee.

The tie kicked off and quite unbelievably North End dominated. Pushing forward throughout the first half hour, Forest hardly had a sniff of a chance near the North End goal...but then again, North End hadn't exactly converted their possession advantage into possibilities on goal either. It was midfield that North End were controlling with some ease, but frustratingly nothing much was happening further up field, bar a handful of half chances, that probably weren't even that.

Spark, Ross, McNab and Cranston were handling anything that Forest could hurl at them, which wasn't much; that was until around the half hour mark.

Then Forest slid into overdrive and started stretching and contorting the North End defence around like a piece of old knicker elastic.

In fact, within just a few minutes of this Forest surge, the home fans thought it was all over for them - twice. First, Ian Storey Moore struck home a shot in breathtaking fashion that left the home fans open mouthed, until the linesman was spotted with his flag raised for offside. It must have been a fractional decision, and the Forest delegation surrounding the ref and his assistant failed to change their minds. Slide rule packed away, the game continued.

In Forest's very next attack, Bob 'Sammy' Chapman had the open goal of all open goals laid before him, but from around a yard out, somehow - *unbelievably* - managed to get his foot under the ball and balloon it over the bar, to the delight of the home fans on the Town End braced waiting for the net to bulge. Perhaps fate was playing a hand here, but North End needed to get things together at the back - and quickly!

Thankfully, Forest didn't quite get over that missed opportunity and the referee soon blew for half time. North End had acquitted themselves well so far. In addition to the home defence, Irvine, Knighton, Lee and Heppolette had ensured they would be mentioned in dispatches.

The game turned North End's way shortly after the resumption - and how! Irvine set the new tempo when his glancing header was saved brilliantly by Peter Grummitt at full stretch.

Six minutes in, Irvine, who had been having a real battle all afternoon with Peter Hindley, had made enough progress with the ball to have arrived inside the Forest box. Hindley unceremoniously gave the Northern Ireland international a distinct shove in the back while trying to deal with the threat he was posing, and the referee had no hesitation in pointing to the penalty spot.

Every North End fan was bouncing now! Up strode Irvine, while the crowd held its breath. I moved through the spectators to get as close as I could behind the Forest net. The whistle blew and he ran in.

Looking at the left hand side of goal as he ran in, Irvine smashed the penalty home off the outside of his right foot - in effect slightly slicing the ball to send Grummitt completely the wrong way. It was a confident shot and unstoppable.

There were no *'we have what we hold'* tactics from North End. With the crowd roaring them on Forest were flustered, and there was further bedlam six minutes later when Temple ran onto a Spark through ball just inside the North End half.

Threaded past Bob McKInlay, the pass enabled Temple to sweep forward quickly, by-pass Terry Hennessy and carry on his fine solo run to around 15 yards from goal. The crowd were screaming in anticipation as his long run ended when he fired in a hard low drive that gave Grummitt no chance. The noise was deafening as Temple turned back to face his team mates who were haring up the field to congratulate him.

The game still had about 30 minutes to go. What a great performance this was turning out to be. Surely, we were going into the next round?

Forest tried to up the tempo just as they had done at the end of the first half, but couldn't make anything happen. The North End defence were rock steady and kept things simple.

With around ten minutes left, North End struck again to put the outcome beyond all doubt.

Hennessy, outstanding for Forest all afternoon, didn't put enough power into a back header directed at Grummitt. As ever, lurking around the scene was the great anticipator, Irvine. Nipping in and taking control of the ball, he was driven wide of the goal when rounding the flailing Grummitt, but the irrepressible centre forward still managed to shoot the ball home from an acute angle.

More joy all round. Why wasn't it like this every week?! The game duly wound down and ended with a youthful pitch invasion and a home crowd pondering, *"where the hell did that performance come from?!"*

Temple said of his goal afterwards, *"Willie (Irvine) was on my right and Gerry (Ingram) on my left, but Hennessy showed me a gap in the middle by moving to the left, where he thought I was going to pass. I had no intention of carrying on until then, but I beat him and found myself in the clear..."*

The Temple goal evoked memories of a similar effort of his in the FA Cup Final of 1966 for Everton against Sheffield Wednesday. In fact, Temple was probably at his peak in '66, as was Willie Irvine, the other source of much Forest pain.

Irvine topped the Division One goal scoring charts in that season when at Burnley. Now three years on, both these 'big match' players had combined to deliver a mortal blow to any Nottingham Forest FA Cup hopes.

*Top: Irvine sends Forest goalkeeper Grummitt the wrong way for the first
Middle: Temple ends a fine solo run by hammering the ball in for the second
Bottom: Irvine rounds Grummitt, eventually shooting home the third from an
acute angle*

32 "I DON'T HAVE A TRAIN TO CATCH..."

PRESTON NORTH END I ASTON VILLA 0
DIVISION TWO 18/1/1969

This was a very wet winter and many of North End's games were postponed as a result. However, it wasn't due to any deluge that on the Saturday immediately following the fantastic display against Nottingham Forest in the FA Cup that Fulham called off their home fixture with North End; it was because too many of their player roster were absent due to the progress of a 'bug' through the club.

The League were sympathetic to their plea and sanctioned their proposal, but not soon enough to prevent North End travelling down for the fixture. Quickly turning around, they travelled back to Manchester to attend the City v Chelsea fixture at Maine Road.

It gave the team a chance to see Chelsea in action, as the Lilywhites had drawn them at home in the FA Cup Fourth Round; due reward for their exploits against Forest.

The following Saturday saw North End welcome Aston Villa to Deepdale. I say *'welcome,'* as by the end of the game, affability was in very short supply!

Tommy Docherty had recently taken over the reins at Villa, and had promptly embarked on run of five wins on the bounce, four in the League and one in the FA Cup. North End had no League form at all to point to; the Forest game being their first win of any kind since November 16th.

On paper, this game had little appeal. Two struggling former giants of the game locked in an unedifying scramble to avoid relegation with at least half a dozen other clubs.

When played, this match-up predictably offered absolutely nothing in terms of football skill - so what makes this poor quality game still sit in a corner of the memory of anyone who witnessed it? Fight, guts and above all justice. That's what!

North End followers who were readers of the Football Post had been prophetically warned about Villa's tactics under 'the Doc' in the letters section of the previous weekend's edition.

Mr P, a North End exile residing in St. Austell, Cornwall, warned that...

"...chaos will rule if team managers employ the survival and success philosophy propounded by Tommy Docherty.

Unfortunately, not only will the image of Villa suffer - also affected without a shadow of a doubt will be the strengths of the clubs with which they will do gladiatorial combat.

Even more alarming is the fact that Docherty is receiving favourable comments from the media. Why do they call him a top man of football? Have they not read the comments of the Carlisle United manager about Docherty's Villa? Did they not read that several of the Villa team were booked at QPR recently?

One can only hope that Preston do not allow themselves to be infected by the 'Docherty Disease' when Villa visit Deepdale next week."

Match day was cold, grey and wet and the pitch was very heavy. With the crowd huddled under whatever cover they could find, North End ran out with the following team :-

Kelly, Ross, McNab, Spavin, Cranston, Heppolette, Temple, Irvine, Ingram, Lee.

It's worth noting at this point that the match referee was Pat Partridge of Middlesbrough, an up and coming referee of some note.

'Enterprising' is the word to describe North End's start to the game, an early neat move down the left resulting in a cross for Ingram that he failed to control on the slippery pitch. Villa demonstrated to the crowd what the remaining 88 minutes were going to be like, as they conceded two free kicks in quick succession, the second producing a lovely rising shot from Knighton that forced John Dunn in the Villa goal to tip over the bar for a corner.

It was ex-Northender Brian Godfrey who drew the first boos of disapproval from the home crowd with his over harassment of Kelly, who was trying to clear the ball.

By now, it was patently apparent that there were two concurrent Villa plans being applied; the first was titled, 'Get Irvine' and the second, 'Foul Anything in White Shirts.' The Villa man-marking was so tight that fouls were committed with ridiculous regularity, and was plainly beginning to upset the North End fans. This wasn't football, it was making fools of the crowd for actually forking out money to watch it. Dour, uncompromising and niggling, it made for difficult watching.

Time and again, a North End player would be felled before even receiving a pass and the crowd were starting to scream at the referee for some sort of action.

All football of any note was coming from North End. Ingram burst through on one occasion, and while leaping clear of a flying tackle, he lost control of the ball and the chance was lost. Irvine assisted with Ingram's next chance but Dunn intercepted the ball and cleared.

Temple set himself up for a shot on goal after a fine solo run, but once again, Dunn was behind the ball at the critical moment.

A rare footballing sortie forward from Peter Broadbent, the noted Villa inside forward, was ended by Spark who regained his feet instantly and fed a pass through to Irvine, inside the Villa half. Making good progress, the centre forward entered the Villa box where he appeared to be completely knocked off his assured stride by Dick Edwards, the visitors centre half. Irvine's resultant stumble meant his shot hit the side netting, but the angry crowd by now were howling for what all present thought was a blatant penalty.

Referee Partridge simply waved play on and the shouts got louder and more abusive.

The crowd had by now firmly taken sides. Anything of the slightest enterprise from North End was met with warm applause and encouragement, as they were genuinely trying to progress in this game.

With the game roughly only 30 minutes old, the Docherty style of play was becoming a serious source of agitation and frustration for the North End fans. They were screaming their disapproval.

The petty and more robust mix of fouls continued; the Villa tactics hitting a new low when Mike Ferguson blatantly hacked down Heppolette after the youngster had waltzed around him in midfield. Predictably this brought deafening protests from the terraces, but the referee only saw fit to lecture Ferguson; the book staying firmly in his back pocket.

'Mastermind' Docherty then introduced another element into the game – blatant time wasting. Brian Tiler, the Villa captain, who had delivered his fair share of fouls, suddenly went down to ground with nobody around him. The 'treatment' seemed to last forever despite the referee chivvying the trainer and Tiler along. The duration of the stoppage was accompanied by shouts and whistles from all corners of Deepdale.

North End attempts on goal were becoming more and more scarce, but the spell was broken when a centre from Ross was met on the full by Ingram, whose header, although saved, drew loud and prolonged applause from the crowd.

Persistent rain was now falling, and if that wasn't bad enough, the totally unpalatable almost happened. In only their third forward movement of the half, Villa manufactured a chance for Broadbent who shot at goal snappily on the turn, initially seeming to send Kelly in the wrong direction. Despite this, the Irishman still managed to twist back in the air and scoop the ball up safely. The Villa attempt on goal drew boos from the crowd, so low was their stock.

North End tried again. Temple, out wide, was pushed beyond the touch line rugby style by Edwards, but from the free kick hit a great shot at goal that Dunn just managed to keep hold of. This brought more warm appreciation for the North End effort.

The next incident saw a return to crowd hostility as Tiler went through the back of Irvine with a Neanderthal tackle that clearly upset the centre forward. Once more, just a ticking off for the defender.

Villa seemed to be pointing to the surface and shrugging their shoulders, implying that this was the reason for the barrage of fouls. It was the dependable Lee's turn next. He was stunned and grounded by an awful tackle that saw him completely lifted off the ground. When Lee eventually regained the strength to walk, he was loudly cheered by the North End fans.

This incident seemed to be the straw that broke the camel's back - for Ross anyway. The next time Villa had the ball, Ross went through Anderson 'Villa-style' to mete out retribution for the tackle on Lee. As the North End patriot made his way back into defence, he too received words of admonishment from the referee, but not booked.

As this unexceptional contest approached half time a brilliant dipping Irvine header was well saved by Dunn to keep the scores level, but in the very last North End forward move of the half, Villa full back Charlie Aitken felled Knighton with an appalling tackle and duly received a much overdue booking from the referee.

It drew the loudest of ironic cheers, in what had been a truly awful display of 'football' by Aston Villa.

Early in the second half, Irvine seized the opportunity to cause mayhem in the unorganised Villa goalmouth, and in the resulting scrum had his shot cleared off the line.

Villa, still not interested in playing football, were continuing to dish out the hard stuff. Tiler was the next name to go into the referees book after he felled Irvine with an uncultured swipe of the leg.

Irvine seemed to be everywhere, and despite the punishment he was receiving was drawing applause from the crowd as he repeatedly drove forward in search of a goal. A long shot from Lee proved harmless, and despite their 'huff and puff' North End were not really showing much imagination in trying to breach the Villa wall. Too many times they ran forward in a gung-ho fashion, only to lose the ball, or be fouled by the Villa spoilers. The crowd didn't desert them though; every move forward of intent was bolstered by the loud encouragement of the home fans.

The Villa time wasting was now really getting out of hand, and Dunn was twice rebuked by Mr.Partridge. During the second lecture, Partridge seemed to gesticulate the message, "fine, carry on then," with a shrug of the shoulders as he ran back down the pitch playing with his watch.

The rain was still driving down but a Knighton volley momentarily lifted the gloom, beating Dunn but agonisingly dropping the wrong side of the post.

The petty time wasting was becoming unbearable for the long suffering spectators, but it appeared that the referee had decided not to waste his breath on lectures any longer, but just adjust his watch accordingly.

The 'contest' was now taking place almost exclusively in the Villa half, with the lone defender Cranston keeping goalkeeper Kelly company. I say 'almost exclusively' as around this time Godfrey broke clear twice and tested Kelly with good shots that demanded his full concentration.

With fifteen minutes left, Irvine was unceremoniously dumped to the floor for the third time in the match, and had to receive prolonged treatment to his knee from the North End trainer.

With time running out, North End ploughed forward (literally, as the pitch was now a mud bath), and Irvine bumped, barged and harassed Villa into conceding a corner to loud cheers from the fans. From the corner, a flare up between Willie Anderson and Temple occurred and Mr. Partridge had to separate the sparring pair like a boxing referee. Temple seemed to be indicating that his heel had been 'raked' and judging from the abusive shouts from the spectators, they agreed with him. Eventually it was all settled, and the game continued...and continued...and continued.

It soon became apparent we were now playing *'Partridge Time!'*

The referee completely ignored the angry 'Doc' on the touchline who was waving his arms and pointing to his watch, as he did the Villa players who kept running up to him on the pitch. The crowd loved it and with renewed vigour, urged North End on.

With well over four minutes of injury time played, Ingram was chopped down on the edge of the Villa box. North End, obviously realising that this 'bonus' time wouldn't last forever, sprinted into position.

Lee floated the ball in, Dunn stretched for the centre but could only push the ball out without any real power and suddenly found his six yard box besieged by white shirts - one of them McNab - who with utmost commitment, slid the ball over the line despite desperate Villa attempts to stop him.

The utter joy of seeing ten North End white shirts celebrate the strike on the Villa goal line was an unforgettable moment after having to put up with all the shenanigans of their tactics. The moment the ball crossed the line, Mr. Partridge raced back to the centre circle and waited for the players to return.

As soon as Villa kicked off, Mr. Partridge blew the full time whistle.

The smiles and delight on the faces of the North End fans belied the fact they had spent good money to watch an appalling game of football. It was a complete and utter paradox.

You couldn't help thinking that we hadn't heard the last of all the goings on, and sure enough the 'Doc' didn't let us down with his post match ramblings of denial and pure fantasy.

Docherty : *"The goal was an injustice. We didn't waste time, the decision by the referee to add time was diabolical; a travesty."*

Seith : *"It was poetic justice that we won it in the added time"*

Docherty : *"We were the better team, man for man, pass for pass."*

Seith : *"The crowd aren't stupid and could see what was behind all the gamesmanship. They encouraged us throughout. Villa's tactics may pay* off from time to time, but it isn't football."

Docherty : *"Irvine deliberately dived to make tackles appear worse than they were - he learned this in the right school didn't he?*

Alan Hubbard (LEP journalist) : *"Doesn't your son play there?!"*

Docherty : *"The worst foul of the match was Irvine on Tiler. He caught him in the mouth with his elbow and knocked his teeth out."*

Seith : *"I spoke to Tiler after the game and he didn't have any teeth missing..."*

Pat Partridge (referee) : *"I felt fully justified in adding on five extra minutes for deliberate time wasting by Villa. I warned their goalkeeper and captain that it had gone on long enough and every second wasted would be added on. I told them that I didn't have a train to catch, and would play until midnight if necessary."*

Bravo!!!

Jim McNab's

After Lee's free kick isn't cleared, the Villa goal is besieged by white shirts, and McNab finally slides the ball over the line, while Irvine halts the progress of the Villa full back

94th minute

With the goal awarded, Irvine congratulates McNab on the floor while their elated team mates (led by Ross and Heppolette) run in to celebrate with them

winner...

Justice finally done! (From left) Knighton, Heppolette, Ross, McNab (back to camera), Ingram, Spark, Irvine (crouching), and Lee

The referee was already waiting at the penalty spot...

33   PENALTY!

PRESTON NORTH END 0 CHELSEA 0
FA CUP 4TH ROUND 25/1/1969

This FA Cup tie was the first of an intriguing mini-series, with the final 'episode' being the classic cliffhanger.

The opener, at Deepdale was by no means an epic, but still very exciting for yours truly, now almost 12 years old.

With 31,875 crammed into the ground, it must have felt like old times to the senior supporters watching from the terraces. On yet another overcast day North End lined up with:-

Kelly, Ross, McNab, Spark, Cranston, Heppolette, Temple, Knighton, Irvine, Ingram and Lee. Substitute: Gemmill.

It was enthralling. The first half was rather like the Forest game in the previous round; North End holding their own but not really creating any clear cut attempts on goal.

The chances that were created were pretty much scrambled affairs.

Mid way through the first half, a Knighton pass down the right wing was put into the crowd by Chelsea full back Stewart Houston as Irvine closed him down. From the throw-in, the ball was controlled in the box by Ingram who chested the ball down and crossed smartly while swiveling on his left foot.

The cross caused mayhem along the six yard line when John Boyle failed to trap the bouncing ball, inviting Lee to fly in at pace and get involved with a challenge; the ball eventually running to Peter Bonetti, who dropped on it gratefully. There were more loud shouts a few minutes later when North End were denied a penalty.

After Temple was accosted by Peter Osgood in midfield, the free kick from Knighton was floated to the back of the six yard box, where Heppolette's leap failed to make contact with the ball. Ingram, however, was alert enough to follow up, stop the ball crossing the by-line and wrap his left foot around it to launch an impromptu cross.

 David Webb the Chelsea centre half, had tracked Ingram back, and as the ball was crossed it plainly stuck his right hand. In fact, the ball hit Webb's outstretched hand so hard it stopped dead behind him, but referee Mr. Burns - stood directly in line with the incident - waved away the penalty claims. Heppolette finally managed to complete the cross, which caused utter pandemonium in the Chelsea box but after two blocked North End shots, Osgood eventually hacked the ball away for a corner with Chelsea struggling to find their bearings.

In the second half, Chelsea came out of their shell, kept North End quiet and displayed their obvious class.

On one occasion, Knighton lost a challenge in the centre circle to Boyle, who quickly fed the ball right to Charlie Cooke. He advanced about 15 yards before unleashing a 30 yard drive all along the ground towards Kelly's bottom right hand corner which the Irish International parried but into the path of Bobby Tambling who promptly drilled the ball back at goal before Ross could complete a tackle. How Kelly managed to get a flick on the ball to deflect it for a corner via the post, nobody will ever know. It was a wonderful effort.

The corner was placed perfectly by Osgood to Webb to run onto and seemingly score with a close range header, but the referee deemed that Tambling had obstructed Kelly's attempt to clear the cross.

A sheepish looking David Webb (extreme left) listens in as Willie Irvine argues for the penalty

Ken Knighton halts the progress of Chelsea's John Boyle

Next it was the formidable Osgood who embarked on a mazy run beating three men but blasting his shot wide of the post. All that occurred right in front of me, and I recall thinking how slick and fast Osgood was. The North End defence didn't even get close to him.

Chelsea had dominated the second half and broke with speed and flair. Their eighth corner of the half had the North End defence hopping around all over the area; the confusion ending when Alan Birchenhall's shot was finally saved by Kelly.

To North End's credit, the match ended goalless, which meant a replay at Stamford Bridge on the following Wednesday evening, and thankfully more gate money for the ailing financial coffers....

34   "PUT THAT LIGHT OUT!"

CHELSEA 2 PRESTON NORTH END 0*
FA CUP 4TH ROUND REPLAY 29/1/1969

(match abandoned after 75 minutes due to floodlight failure)

As a North End fan, I was used to seeing opposition teams let off the hook by our poor finishing. However, what transpired on this particular evening was a massive payback for all those previous disappointments!

Ingram was replaced by Spavin for 'episode two', North End fielding :-

Kelly, Ross, McNab, Spark, Cranston, Heppolette, Temple, Spavin, Irvine, Knighton and Lee. Substitute: Gemmill.

It was the 'rabbits caught in the headlights' North End that turned up at Stamford Bridge that night.

Hardly able to compete with the home team, who were being roared on by most of the 44,239 crowd, it seemed like the standard 'disect and destroy' Chelsea procedure would be more than enough to trot into the fifth round without even breaking sweat.

In fact, seeing North End actually in the opposition half was a bonus. Chelsea had hammered away at the visitors goal for most of the 35 minutes it took them to score. It was akin to watching jovial people pegging away at the fairground coconut shy on Preston Flag Market on a sunny Bank Holiday afternoon.

Ian Hutchinson scored the opener, his first ever goal for Chelsea. He had just moved to Chelsea from non-league Cambridge United and was the transfer bargain of 1968/69, costing just £2,000.

He was having a good and fair tussle with Cranston, but the big North End centre half wasn't quick enough when Hutchison ran towards Cooke's floated corner and superbly glanced his header back and across Kelly and into the net.

It was another Cooke corner in the 52nd minute that led to Chelsea's second. The ball wasn't cleared and Birchenhall's snap half volley from around six yards out hit the net before Kelly hit the floor.

Effectively, game over.

However, on 74 minutes the flood lights suddenly dimmed to around or below half power. The referee stopped play, and after consulting a club official in the players tunnel, decided to carry on. That eye straining experience lasted just two further minutes before more of the lights failed causing another stoppage to play.

There were more consultations, with the players hanging around on the pitch chatting to each other. Then came the announcement that the problem could not be fixed, and the tie had been abandoned.

Spavin, Gemmill, Knighton, Heppolette and Temple 'mingle' with the Chelsea players whilst officials search for a shilling for the meter

Chelsea announced later that the match would take place on February 3rd at 7:30pm, or if the floodlights were still in a state of disrepair - at

3pm in the afternoon.

The statement from Chelsea read,

"The cause of the blaze was a fire in the electrical junction box that served the floodlights. The cable involved had three cores, all separated by pitch to keep them apart. When the cable overheated, the pitch melted, the cores touched and the fire started. The blaze was promptly dealt with but nothing could be immediately done to enable the match to be completed."

All this gave plenty of scope for comment in the bleak 'Colditz' (secondary school) playground .

Immediately the hopeful notion floated by the loyalists that North End may win next time out against Chelsea, was waved away with indignation by those self styled 'knowledgeable' kids who had 'moved on' to support Everton, (a big team back then), and Manchester United.

Me? After the way they had shaped in this encounter I expected North End to lose, but stranger things had happened in football....

FRONT PAGE SPORT

SPAVIN — "On Monday it could be our turn." SEXTON — "Of course we're disappointed." SMITH — "Happy to have another chance."

❛ Someone up there loves us ❜

Preston just light up with laughter!

It was a happy North End that arrived back from London. Floodlight failure had given them another chance in this cup tie – could they really pull off a miracle next time?

35   NEARLY, BUT NOT QUITE

CHELSEA 2 PRESTON NORTH END 1
FA CUP 4TH ROUND REPLAY 3/2/1969

So to the last game of this trilogy, and the most gripping of the three.

After yet another away defeat in Division Two against Bristol City by 2-1, North End limped into London for the Monday afternoon 'replay of the replay' licking their wounds.

Willie Irvine, suffering from suspected knee ligament trouble following a tackle by Webb in the Deepdale encounter was a definite non-starter. He had played through the pain barrier in the abandoned game, but the injury had now worsened.

Arsenal offered their Highbury facilities for North End to run fitness tests on McNab and Cranston who unfortunately were deemed unfit to play after picking up knocks at Ashton Gate. This meant an immediate reshuffling of the team, and North End ran out into the cold winter sunshine with the following team :-

Kelly, Ross, Knighton, Spark, Hawkins, Heppolette, Temple, Spavin, Ingram, Gemmill, Lee. Substitute : Lloyd

The crowd managed to reach 36,522 - remarkable for a 'working day' afternoon, and Chelsea soon had them cheering by making the early running. Chelsea seemed to be playing with a lot more urgency than in the previous encounters, and soon North End were pushed back deep into their own half, leaving just Temple and Ingram upfield.

Charlie Cooke looked 'on-song' and was having a real battle against fellow Scot, Ross. After seeing the full back curtail one menacing run, he then got the better of him and fed the ball to Tambling, whose cross was well cut out by Kelly.

Hawkins, enjoying his first game back after an injury lay off was imposing himself well on Birchenhall, and generally North End began to grow in confidence.

A neat little move involving the tireless Gemmill put Lee through but he lost control of the ball in the penalty area. On 11 minutes another break forward earned the visitors a corner after a free kick by Knighton had been headed on by Heppolette; Bonetti being happy to push the ball safely over the bar.

Heppolette then sent Temple racing towards goal, but Houston conceded a corner in safety-first fashion. He wished he hadn't!

Lee floated the corner in beautifully, Temple hung in the air and glanced the ball onwards across the face of goal, and Ingram racing in headed it into the net from close range. It was a lovely goal.

Temple (left) leaps above the Chelsea defence to glance the ball on for Ingram (hidden by no.4, Spark) to head home

The touch paper was now well and truly lit. After coasting through the first two meetings, Chelsea were suddenly under pressure and panic was certainly visible in their play.

North End on the other hand, were seemingly enjoying this challenge. The defence stood firm under the guidance of Hawkins, and even put some enterprising moves together of their own. Chelsea couldn't get near the North End box, and clearly Bobby Seith had formulated 'a plan.'

Lee and Gemmill were working very hard too, moving forwards and backwards and getting involved when necessary.

Chelsea were becoming irritated that they couldn't pierce the North End shield, and started niggling with cheap fouls. Boyle earned a talking too from the referee for a bad foul on Temple, the former Evertonian – who had to receive prolonged treatment from the trainer.

Hawkins brought more frustration for the home side when Hollins cleverly ducked under a Cooke centre with the intent of letting it through to Birchenhall behind him, but the North End marshal had spotted the move, chesting down the interception and clearing upfield.

Just after the half hour, Kelly did have to come to the rescue, however.

Hollins crossed on the run for Osgood who met the ball well with his head, forcing the North End 'keeper to leap and bend backwards spectacularly to pull the ball down.

CHELSEA STUNNED BY SHOCK INGRAM GOAL

Chelsea were throwing the kitchen sink at North End's defence, but with the advantage in their back pocket, the Lilywhites were fighting just as tigerishly to keep them at bay.

Chelsea didn't like it, and their famed 'hard men' started meting out the rough stuff. Within the space of a few minutes, those sterling workhorses Lee and Gemmill were uncompromisingly dealt with.

Lee needed a session with the trainer after being poleaxed by a McCreadie tackle, as did Gemmill – who was clutching the back of his knee in agony after a 'brush' with Ron Harris.

The frantic play of the hosts was in direct contrast to the cool methodical way Spavin was running the North End midfield. Unruffled by Chelsea's antics, he set off a lovely move between himself, Ross and Temple that opened up their hosts at the back, but ended when the winger shot over the bar.

There was one last salvo from Chelsea before half time, which almost rewarded them with the equaliser.

Tambling breached the North End barrier, latching on to a nod through from Birchenhall but his shot, although beating Kelly, grazed the outside of the post and went for a goal kick.

Half time arrived with North End still intact. I was just about leaving school at this point, wondering just how the team were going on in an age where there was no instant access to football news. I wouldn't be home in time for the 4:15 Sports Desk on the radio, so the best bet was likely to be the television news just before 6 o'clock. A long time to wait!

The second half got underway, and Chelsea were still frantically attacking the North End goal.

Osgood and Tambling went close, before the latter burst clear of the North End back line, leaving just Kelly to beat. It appeared as though he had when Kelly opted to dive in the wrong direction, but somehow managed to get his legs to the ball and it bounced away to safety.

A couple of minutes later, Tambling missed an absolute sitter, slicing wide after being set up by a short Osgood pass.

The most unlikely player on the pitch was then at the centre of a flare up between the two teams. Spavin tripped Osgood in midfield which provoked a massive overreaction from the *'King of Stamford Bridge.'* McCreadie then got involved, but the referee managed to diffuse the situation as the North End defenders appeared on the scene to lend 'Spav' some support.

However there was still a lot of finger wagging directed at the referee from the Preston team.

Birchenhall then streaked forward but could only push his final shot across the face of goal after being driven wide by Ross. Boyle then rammed in a 20 yard effort but it was too high. Within a few moments it was Boyle again - on this occasion heading over the angle of post and bar from a right wing cross.

Osgood had another chance but was well wide and then Hawkins conceded a corner after blocking a Tambling shot.

North End could just not move forward and as the siege continued, Ingram was re-located to a spot in defence behind Hawkins. It immediately paid dividends as the big striker hooked away a dangerous ball crossing the goalmouth.

On the hour, it was Gemmill, that midfielder with the everlasting batteries who so, so nearly settled this game once and for all. Chelsea were at absolute desperation point and had pushed every available body forward to lay siege to the North End goal.

This left them alarmingly open and when Gemmill gained possession, raced away and smashed a glorious shot through Bonetti's hands, for just an instant the whole of Chelsea thought that was it. Cruelly for North End - and Gemmill - the ball cannoned downwards off the bar, bounced in front of the goal line and was collected by the shaken Chelsea 'keeper.

On it continued. Chelsea without doubt should have scored and would have scored but for North End's superb tight marking and fluid defence.

People were starting to drift away from the stadium, and incredibly as the clock ticked past the 90th minute, North End were still in front. It was then that the most cruel of match turning incidents happened.

Ross went down injured after being apparently fouled, and the ball then ran out of play for a throw in. No foul was awarded and with Ross writhing in agony on the floor the referee ignored pleas to let the North End trainer on the pitch to attend to him.

Chelsea motored forward while Ross trailed behind them hobbling and holding his leg. It was to no avail.

Webb, who had been thrown into attack in desperation when Chelsea hopes were fading as fast as their floodlights had in the previous encounter, had a shot cleared off the North End goal line. The ball came out to Boyle - and his back heel was cleared off the line. Eventually it was Birchenhall who headed the ball back towards Webb, who then nodded home the equaliser into the right hand corner despite Kelly's flailing attempt.

If that wasn't heartbreaking enough, there was to be no extra time...

Almost straight from the kick off North End conceded possession and found themselves in pursuit of Birchenhall who ran down the left. With Kelly beaten, his cross-cum-shot was helped over the line by Cooke arriving full pelt just ahead of Gemmill.

Chelsea, with two goals in the last 90 seconds had stolen the fifth round of the FA Cup from Preston - literally! North End trooped off demoralised and not one of the team looked up from the floor on that slow walk back to the dressing room, as Chelsea fans swarmed onto the pitch.

Around this time, I was pulling the Evening Post through the letterbox, and being startled to see the back page headline, 'CHELSEA STUNNED BY SHOCK INGRAM GOAL.' I couldn't believe it, and was hoping against hope that we had hung on. Being stuck in a 'time warp' isn't easy...

Left: Webb's header beats Kelly for the Chelsea equaliser

Right: A few moments later, Cooke slams home the winner

I think I must have looked as gutted as the North End players did later that night. In the hour it took to hear the final score read out on television, I must have read the back page of the newspaper tens of times, each time convincing myself that North End would do it. Alas it wasn't to be…

The following morning a friend told me on the school bus that his uncle had been to the game and that he and his dad collected him from Preston Railway Station in the evening. Details were a little sketchy but the word was that Chelsea's tackling *"was dirty to say the least"* and the referee did nothing about it.

This seemed to be borne out when the *Evening Post* dropped through the letter box just before five o' clock, complete with reaction to the game.

Describing North End as *'PROUD BUT ANGRY'* the article went on to say that Bobby Seith was full of praise for his team, but not the referee.

"George Ross went down injured after being fouled and the ball went out of play for a throw-in. He was rolling around from a knock to the knee and with cramp on top of all that, but the referee would not let Walter Crook (the trainer) onto the field to attend to him. Play carried on and Chelsea got their equaliser, which would never had happened if George had been fit. He limped back heroically to try and get into position but couldn't and Webb's header went in where he would have been covering in normal circumstances. It was the most important incident of the match - George was not shamming and as a team we never wasted time. There was a proliferation of over the ball tackling. Frank Lee took a tremendous amount of punishment yesterday, as did Derek Temple and Gerry Ingram."

Then it was the turn of the North End players to offer a litany of quotes. With so many of the players saying the same thing, it is hard not to have sympathy with their side of the story…

"The end of the game brought me nearer to tears than ever before. I just can't get over it. The Cup Final was bad enough but this was beyond belief"
George Ross

217

"Eddie McCreadie fouled me every time he made a tackle. I thought we played some fine football but they are a team who cannot take defeat and they went mad in the second half."
Frank Lee

"Our defence was tremendous without ever resorting to the tactics Chelsea used. They went over-the-ball all the time."
Derek Temple

"Chelsea were allowed to get away with it. We played cleanly throughout the game, but Harris was vicious. He even hit Ricky and myself in the face"
Gerry Ingram

"It was terrible, I can't believe it. I was sickened by the result and had just started to look forward to playing Stoke in the next round."
Ricky Heppolette

"Every time I got the ball they hammered me. It certainly wasn't football but the referee never even warned them."
Alan Spavin

"The ref let Chelsea get away with murder."
Ken Knighton

"Chelsea's tactics would never have been allowed in a normal Second Division game."
Graham Hawkins

"We were smiling last week but I could have cried for the lads this time."
Jim McNab *(injured, watching from the bench)*

We can confidently add Willie Irvine's knee damage that was to keep him out of action for a long spell to the list above, which was, as mentioned previously, the direct result of a harsh Webb challenge at Deepdale.

It all seems to point to yet another of those football occasions when the 'big team' is treated rather differently to the 'little team' in a one-off match. It has happened since time immemorial; still goes on today, and nobody quite knows why.

If the referee had given the blatant handball against Webb at Deepdale perhaps there would have been no need for a replay. One thing is certain; if the situation had been in reverse, it *would* have been a penalty...

36   GEMMILL'S GAME

PRESTON NORTH END 2 LEICESTER CITY 1
DIVISION TWO 11/10/1969

This was the occasion when the 14,492 fortunate enough to have been present witnessed *'Gemmill's Game.'* It was a glimpse of what was waiting just around the corner for Archie, and what an absolute treat it was!

In the previous weeks, North End had hit a patch where, despite playing reasonably well, just couldn't score. They came into this game with just ten points from their 13 games, placing them fifth from bottom. The real alarm was that they had found the onion bag on just eight occasions, but, had positively countered that by only conceding ten goals themselves. This ranked the North End defence as the second best in Division Two.

Leicester City were flying high, looking to regain their Division One status. They were tracking the leaders in fourth place with 18 points from their 13 games and boasted players of real quality in their squad. The real nugget of gold within those ranks was a youthful Peter Shilton, who was at the very start of a glittering club and later, international career.

North End fielded a well balanced team for this game :-

Kelly, Ross, Ritchie, Heppolette, Hawkins, McNab, Wilson, Spavin, Gemmill and Temple. Substitute : Ingram

Early North End promise was accompanied by a goodwill message from the goal starved home fans, who reworked John Lennon and Yoko Ono's monster hit with the chant, *"All we are saying is ... give us a goal."*

North End were certainly trying. Temple, Gemmill and Wilson combined well and Wilson was stopped at the expense of a corner. This was punched out by Shilton, but Ross was on hand to hammer the ball back into the box which Gemmill headed on and the keeper did well to save.

City - without both of their free scoring forwards, Andy Lochhead and Rodney Fern - then came into the game, with some neat approach work leading to shots on target from both full back David Nish and roving winger Len Glover.

This was settling into a very watchable contest, played at a fast pace with City very swift on the counter. Hawkins, commanding his space well, saw to it that two such potentially dangerous situations were dealt with efficiently and with skill. The defence always looked assured when the ex-Wolves player led the back line.

It was North End though who were 'bossing' this game, and noticeably crossing at every possible occasion, giving the forwards ample opportunity to bump and barge the young Shilton - presumably to put the youngster off his game.

The crowd applauded loudly when Temple fired in a curling, rising shot that skimmed the top of Shilton's crossbar, but had even more to cheer after 25 minutes.

Irvine, unexpectedly for the Leicester defence, volleyed a superb, defence splitting pass direct to Temple on the left wing. With the City defenders taken by surprise, Temple then added to their woes by crossing the ball quickly and accurately, seeking out the supercharged Gemmill hurtling in to head past Shilton for North End's opener. The enterprise and execution of the move were perfect, and the crowd encouraged North End noisily.

Gemmill, who had been buzzing all over the pitch then provided Irvine with a chance, but Shilton somehow managed to narrow the angle and save his low shot.

It was all Preston now, and indeed 'all Gemmill,' as the human dynamo hit a screaming long drive that had Shilton flying across his goal to save.

Leicester retaliated and another rapid team break saw Glover arrow a shot just over the bar with Kelly well beaten.

There was still enough time left though for two more scintillating, supercharged, mazy runs from that man Gemmill, that didn't produce any goals, but did produce long appreciative applause from the crowd.

The 'wee man' walked briskly off the pitch at half time, and was obviously on a mission. For all his lack of height, he must have felt ten feet tall.

Archie Gemmill celebrates his, and North End's first goal against Leicester City

The second half commenced and Gemmill, with batteries recharged, was promptly at it again.

He forced his way down the left, creating an opening for Temple who shot wide. He then sprayed an inch perfect crossfield ball to the feet of Wilson, who quickly moved forward and centered into the area where Gemmill, following the move into the box at speed, headed just wide.

Irvine then went close with a header from a Wilson corner before Gemmill went even closer after his sheer speed spread-eagled the City defence following a one-two with Spavin.

North End continued to camp in the Leicester half, and Irvine hammered in a shot that saw Shilton make the save of the day, contorting his body to palm the ball past the post.

Then Wilson, after beating his marker on the right took the ball no further forward, instead passing the ball inside into the surging Gemmill's path; the visitors escaping as Peter Rodrigues managed to clear the resulting shot off the goal line with Shilton beaten.

The North End attacks towards the Kop end continued unabated and on 65 minutes, North End went 2-0 up. It was another Gemmill gem; a quite unbelievable goal to lend credence to all those who say, *"anything is achievable."*

A long, hopeful punt from Ross into the Leicester box was harming nobody until John Sjoberg and Shilton got into one unholy mess over who was looking after the ball. Shilton had ventured well forward off his line and was behind the completely unaware Sjoberg, who continued with a back header in the direction of where he thought Shilton still was.

The ball slid past Shilton, but was retrievable with a sprint. Gemmill was already on his way. Spotting the potential mix up, he had set off like a bullet from fully 40 yards from City's goal, and the crowd watched the developing outcome with a mixture of open mouths and yelps of anticipation.

Within a matter of seconds, Gemmill was neck and neck with Shilton and launched his left foot at the ball, managing to squeeze it over the line - the ball running gently into the opposite corner as Shilton looked on aghast. Gemmill's impetus saw him slide over the touchline via the post, coming to rest facing his team running towards him to celebrate.

The standing ovation lasted almost until City kicked off again. A superhuman effort, from a quite unique player.

Shell shocked City then had to thank Graham Cross for clearing an Irvine header off the line, as North End tried to add to their tally.

Leicester persevered, and lady luck finally smiled on them when after a

Main Picture : Gemmill wins the race with Shilton to score a quite unbelievable opportunist goal...

Inset : ...and his impetus propels him over the touchline and next to the goal stanchions

quick breakaway, winger Paul Matthews fired in a shot that hit Kelly's post; the rebound being calmly slotted home by Alistair Brown before the keeper could regain himself. There were still 18 minutes to go; surely North End wouldn't let this game slip?

Leicester piled on some pressure in what was easily their best spell of the match, but in a moment I recall well, the final whistle blew as 'Go-Go' Gemmill was symbolically powering forward with the ball just as he had been at the very start.

Deepdale, or any other ground in England for that matter, had never seen anything like Gemmill before - nor have they since. His effort and devotion to the North End cause were undeniable; his style stirring and inspirational. Young and old in the crowd thoroughly enjoyed his weekly committed performance. He was revered - a unique player - and we all followed his subsequent top class career with sense of pride that he once graced the Deepdale pitch in North End's colours.

Show stopper

PNE's star—

● Peter Shilton the Leicester 'keeper, punches clear a ball from Ross during today's game at Deepdale.

'Educated Archie!'

By NORMAN SHAKESHAFT

AN AGGRESSIVE, almost cocky Preston North End, played their best football of the season, at Deepdale this afternoon, in trying to add to a one goal lead they established over promotion challenging Leicester City, in the 24th minute.

ARCHIE GEMMILL Scored after 24 minutes to put North End ahead.

37   NORTH END FANTASY TEAM OF THE SIXTIES?

Picking a 'North End Team of the Sixties' is a well nigh impossible task, as some top footballing talent graced Deepdale in that decade. Everybody will have a different opinion.

I started watching North End from the mid sixties onwards, so have to rely on reports and other fan's testimonials for performances before then.

I have picked what I think is a team that, if all were *fit and at their peak* today, would easily compete with many of today's *'superstars.'*

Kelly

Ross   Singleton   Kendall   McNab

Lawton (captain)

Wilson   Gemmill   Thompson

Dawson   Irvine

Substitutes (*any three from*):-

Barton, Godfrey, Hannigan, Hawkins, Knighton, Smith/Lyall, Spavin.

Manager: Jimmy Milne

Alan Kelly was the first choice goalkeeper throughout the decade for North End, as well as establishing himself as a Republic of Ireland international. **George Ross** and **Jim McNab** were the most effective pairing of full backs that North End had enjoyed for some time. Both were effective in the tackle and counter attack, and both were 'footballers.' **Tony Singleton** was like a rock in the middle of the defence for the best part of the decade; unforgiving in the tackle, and also the back line 'organiser.' **Howard Kendall,** composed in defence, was naturally gifted in art of attack too, and a quite superb talent.

Early in their Preston careers, both **David Wilson** and **Peter Thompson** were capped at England U23 level, and in my world, it would be unthinkable to exclude them from the team. These caps were not handed out like chocolate bars for Division Two players. You had to be *exceptional.* Fast, tricky and full of pace, North End would be able to open up most flanks with these two on board. In the middle has to be **Nobby Lawton**, who is also my captain. He provided real inspiration; cajoling and demanding his players to perform. On top of that you always got a quality performance, linking the back and front lines tirelessly. Alongside him, is **Archie Gemmill** - but it could just as well be Alan Spavin. I have given Gemmill the nod particularly for his obvious fetching and carrying skills, speed and passion to win any game of football, and the fact he became a regular full international.

Alex Dawson and **Willie Irvine** lead the attack, and I envisage hatfuls of goals going in with their no-nonsense approach to goal scoring. I also see them feeding of each other's play. Both of these players have outstanding career records, which were achieved under much harder conditions than forwards enjoy today. I'm sure it would have been a great partnership.

John Barton, more than capable, covered for Kelly more than anyone else in the sixties, so is the substitute goalkeeper. **Brian Godfrey** was a polished goal scorer and later in his career successfully converted into a midfield general. **Ernie Hannigan** was exceptional on the right wing and unlucky to be on the bench, and it's only fact that **Graham Hawkins** arrived at Deepdale near the end of the decade that he is sitting on his hands alongside him. His prime time was just around the corner. **Ken Knighton** was a real defender 'for the cause' who also possessed a cannonball shot, and **Jim Smith** was a stalwart who could cover most defensive areas. **George Lyall** came to North End from Raith Rovers in 1966, when a youngster. He was a more than useful goalscoring midfielder, yet another player with a hammer shot who could pass accurately and win the ball in a tackle. That brings me to **Alan Spavin**, he of the precision pass, the intelligent reading of a situation, the unwavering loyalty to his club. I find it hard now to even consider putting him being on the bench...so let's say that if the Lawton/Gemmill partnership doesn't work, 'Spav' is straight in!

Manager Jimmy Milne watching intently alongside trainer Walter Crook and substitute George Lyall in November 1967.

38   RESEARCH & RESTORATION

It seems that very few action pictures of North End in the sixties – and indeed the seventies - survived the *Lancashire Evening Post* move from Fishergate in the city centre to Fulwood; in fact many of the pictures in this book have had to be painstakingly recovered from aged, heavily worn and score damaged microfilm records. Other than that I have been very grateful to use actual participants scrapbooks, or indeed my own.

To relate the story of North End over a decade, I wanted to be able to illustrate a scene or specific moment and how the event was reported or depicted to the fans, and while seeing a photograph spring back to life after hours of restoration is very satisfying; it is still not an original...but I did my best!

During the long hours of research, the appropriate piece of microfilm had to be photographed from the monitor display, transferred to computer, then painstakingly processed by appropriate software. Some microfilm photographs just could not be improved. Many hours were wasted trying to lift the image profile only to have to throw the towel in half way through. The written word wasn't any easier to see either.

An example of a restoration is on the next page. It's a tragedy, as the quality of the *Lancashire Evening Post's* reporting of all aspects relating to North End was exceptional to say the least. Not only were the club promoted to the public in every single issue, the quality of the journalists employed by the *Post* was second to none. Fleet Street's Steve Curry, Joe Melling and Alan Hubbard all started at the *'Post'* and reported on North End games at some point, not forgetting of course Walter Pilkington and latterly Norman Shakeshaft.

I asked Steve Curry how he liked working in Fishergate in the early sixties, *"Really enjoyed it. I was asked to go back later, but by then was already in Fleet Street."*

The microfilm of the *Football Post* front page of 14/3/1964, as viewed on monitor...

...following extensive processing, a much cleaner image.

39   SCRAPBOOK

Deciding which images to finally use with the main text was difficult, and inevitably has resulted in a few omissions. Rather than see these pictures be locked away and remain unseen, this is a good opportunity to showcase them as they capture the Sixties era well.

All of the following pictures were either recovered through software processing or digitally copied from old scrapbooks.

October 1961   **Preston North End 0 Sunderland 1**
Sunderland centre half Charlie Hurley beats North End's Alfie Biggs to the ball following a cross. Brian Clough watches on (extreme right).

February 1962   **Preston North End 1 Derby County 0**

A Derby County shot passes North End's John Wylie (centre) towards goal, but was saved by 'keeper Alan Kelly

August 1962   **Preston North End 2 Norwich City 2**

After weaving his way through the Norwich defence, David Wilson is robbed at the last moment

December 1962   **Preston North End 1 Chelsea 3**

After working his way down the left, Chelsea's Bobby Tambling (obscured by the post), sends in a hard low shot that beats 'keeper Alan Kelly. Watching on (from left), are David Barber, Barry Bridges (Chelsea), Tony Singleton and John Donnelly

December 1963   **Preston North End 0 Leyton Orient 0**

Alan Kelly safely catches a cross from Malcolm Musgrove of Leyton Orient in the opening minutes of the game. George Ross is the defender in the foreground

February 1964　　　　　　**Huddersfield Town 2 Preston North End 2**

A jubilant Howard Kendall, after Doug Holden (not in picture) had scored North End's first goal

March 1964　　　　　　**Preston North End 2 Manchester City 0**

Brian Godfrey (obscured by the post), shoots from the corner of the penalty box giving the advancing Bert Trautmann no chance when scoring North End's second goal

SAFELY GATHERED IN ...

October 1964   **Preston North End 2 Swindon Town 1**

*John Barton collects the ball from a header. George Ross, Nobby Lawton and
Tony Singleton are the closest North End defenders*

INTO THE MISTS OF DEEPDALE

December 1964   **Preston North End 1 Crystal Palace 0**

*John Barton punches away a Palace cross at the last moment with David Payne
challenging. George Ross and Tony Singleton are the North End defenders.*

February 1965   **Preston North End 2 Newcastle United 0**

David Wilson waltzes around Frank Clark, the Newcastle United full back

February 1965   **Preston North End 2 Derby County 2**

Brian Godfrey's header from an Alan Spavin cross goes just wide of the post.
David Wilson is also in attendance.

September 1965   **Leyton Orient 2 Preston North End 2**

Alan Spavin and Brian Godfrey pursue 15 year old Leyton Orient protégé, Paul Went

April 1968   **Blackburn Rovers 0 Preston North End 1**

Willie Irvine (centre, partly obscured) slams home a penalty to ruin Easter for Rovers. Archie Gemmill, Ken Knighton and Ray Charnley look on.

August 1968   **Cardiff City 1 Preston North End 0**

Alan Kelly manages to cut out a Cardiff City cross at Ninian Park. The Cardiff players are Brian Clark (8) and John Toshack; the North End defenders are Jim Smith, Graham Hawkins (5) and George Ross (obscured by Hawkins).

September 1969   **Preston North End 2 Sheffield United 1**

Archie Gemmill's flying interception attempt just fails as Alan Hodgkinson, the 'Blades' goalkeeper just manages to grasp the ball.

PICTURE KEY – FRONT COVER

Left
Archie Gemmill in action against Sheffield United, September 1969.

Centre
Tony Singleton heads North End's equaliser against Man Utd, March 1966.

Right
Alex Dawson foraging in the Sunderland penalty area, January 1963.

PICTURE KEY – BACK COVER

Top
'Old Deepdale' in all its glory for the first game of the season against Rotherham United in August 1964.

Bottom section – from top left, clockwise
Alan Kelly in action at Villa Park in November, 1968.

The Preston North End special edition programme v Chelsea in January 1969.

Tom Finney shakes hands with the Luton Town captain before his final game.

Brian Godfrey turns away after scoring v Manchester City, November 1964.

The 'Last Football' Post front page headline, March 5th 1966.

The Preston North End first team squad, (minus Howard Kendall) 1963/64.

Archie Gemmill powers In a header against Leicester City, October 1969.

North End v Swansea Town FA Cup semi final toss up at Villa Park, March 1964.

Nobby Lawton leads out North End at Oxford in the FA Cup, February 1964.

Alex Dawson at the Oxford pre match kick-in.

Jim Smith calmly clears the West Ham danger in the FA Cup final, May 1964.

(Centre) Willie Irvine rounds the Forest keeper before scoring, January 1969.

By the same Author…

Available from: **www.amazon.co.uk**

Printed in Poland
by Amazon Fulfillment
Poland Sp. z o.o., Wrocław